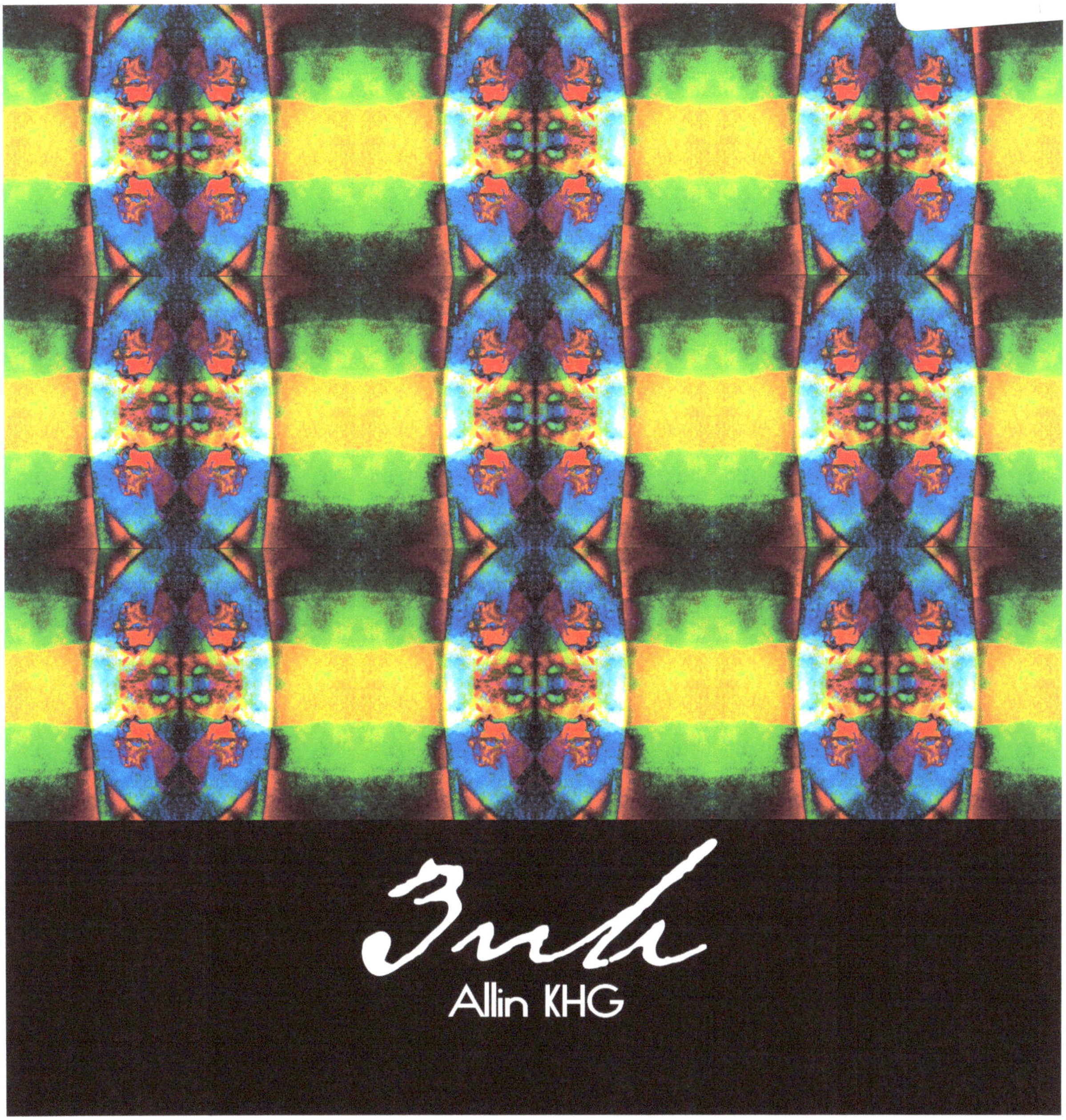

3nli

Allin KHG

3nh

by
Allin KHG

2014
KHG InterServ
Oklahoma City, OK
empallin@yahoo.com

For Samantha

Thank You For Everything

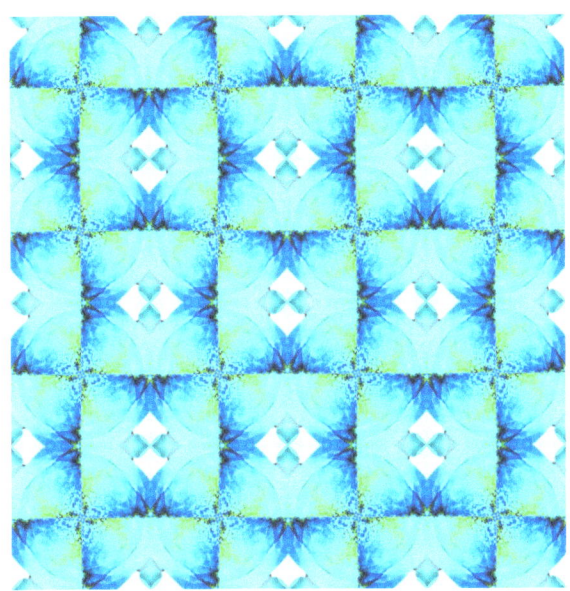

A Quick Introduction

The images in this collection were an experiment in random pattern making with the use of photo manipulation. Each image started as a photograph. The photograph was overlaid on top of itself at a rotated angle. The image was then laid out in a repeating pattern to show how I originally intended them to be viewed.

The images are presented with different amounts of repeating to show the changes in the way they look at different sizes. There are a few that are identical except for color. The color changes affect the appeal but not the actual appearance.

When I started working on these I thought they would be interesting as wallpaper. Though I am not opposed to that now, the final images seem like they would be too bold and busy for that use. They could still work as fabric, but that is completely different. Personally I just like them as they are presented here.

This started out as just a fun little attempt to make something different and interesting out of some of the pictures I had. The final results far exceeded my expectations. I am not really sure what I expected, but some of these are absolutely beautiful to me. I can only hope they are half as interesting and attractive to you, the viewer.

Thanks to Sara Young and Alexandra Vecchiolla for editorial assistance.

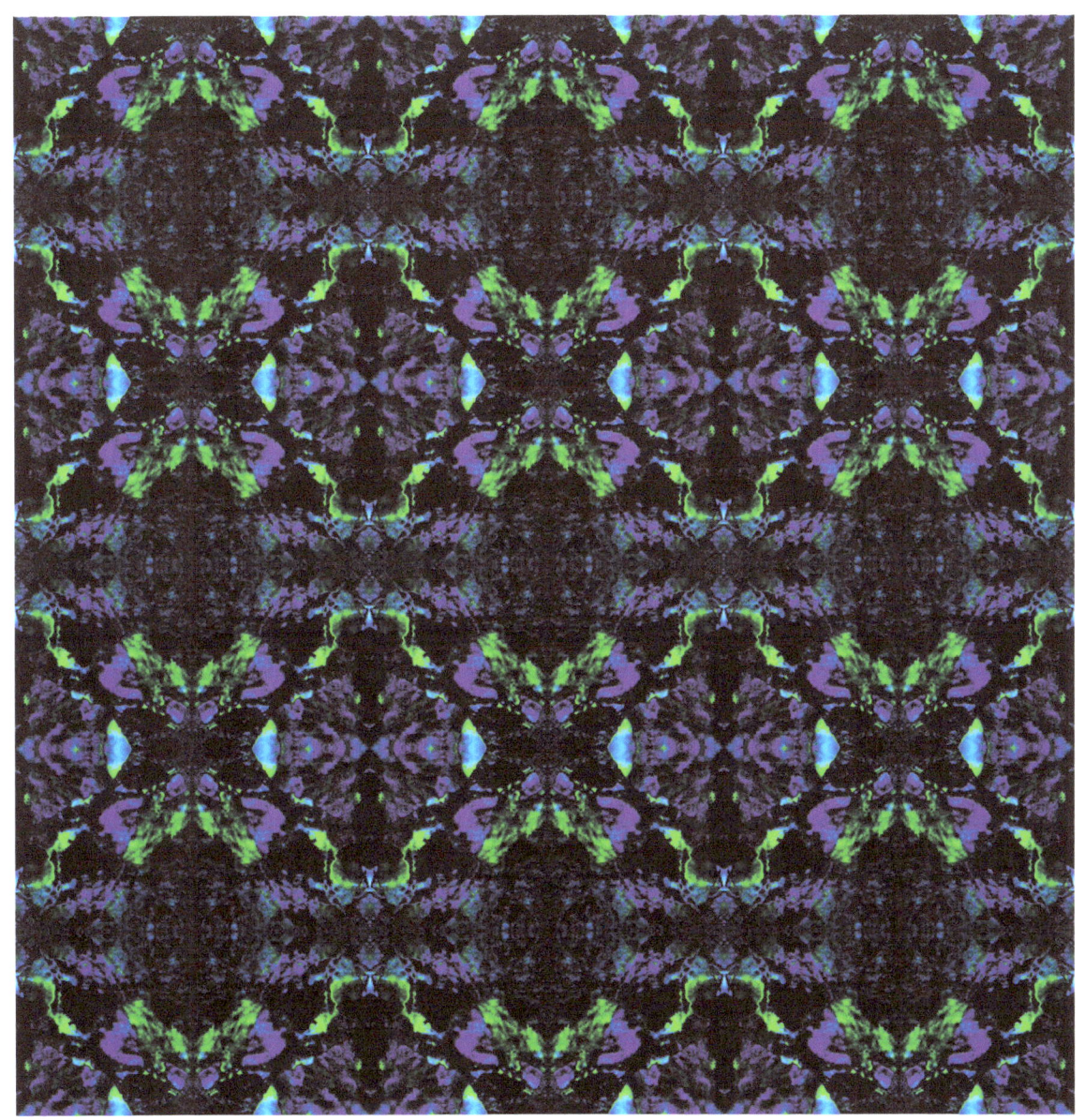

A Few Things

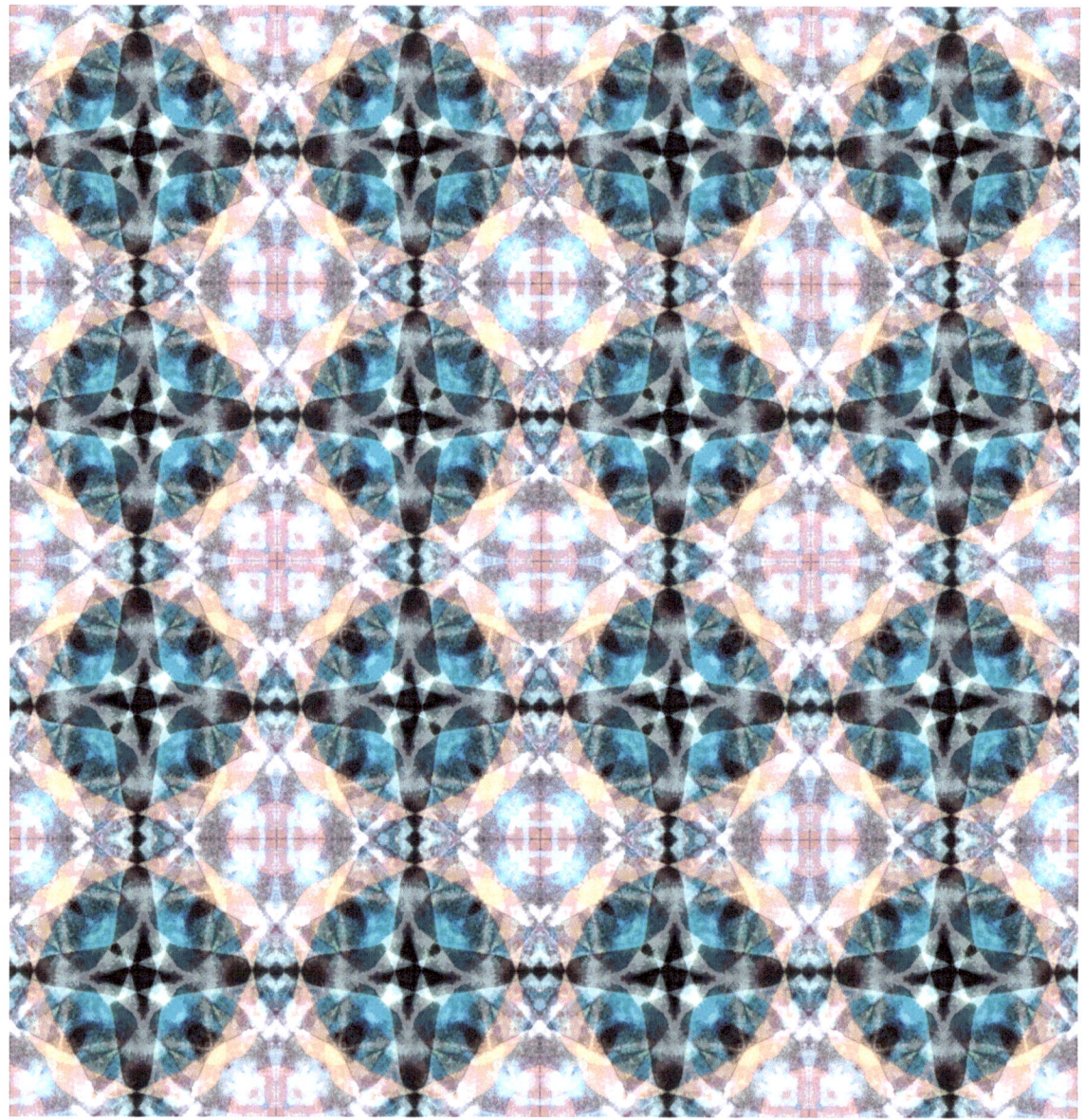

A Pain

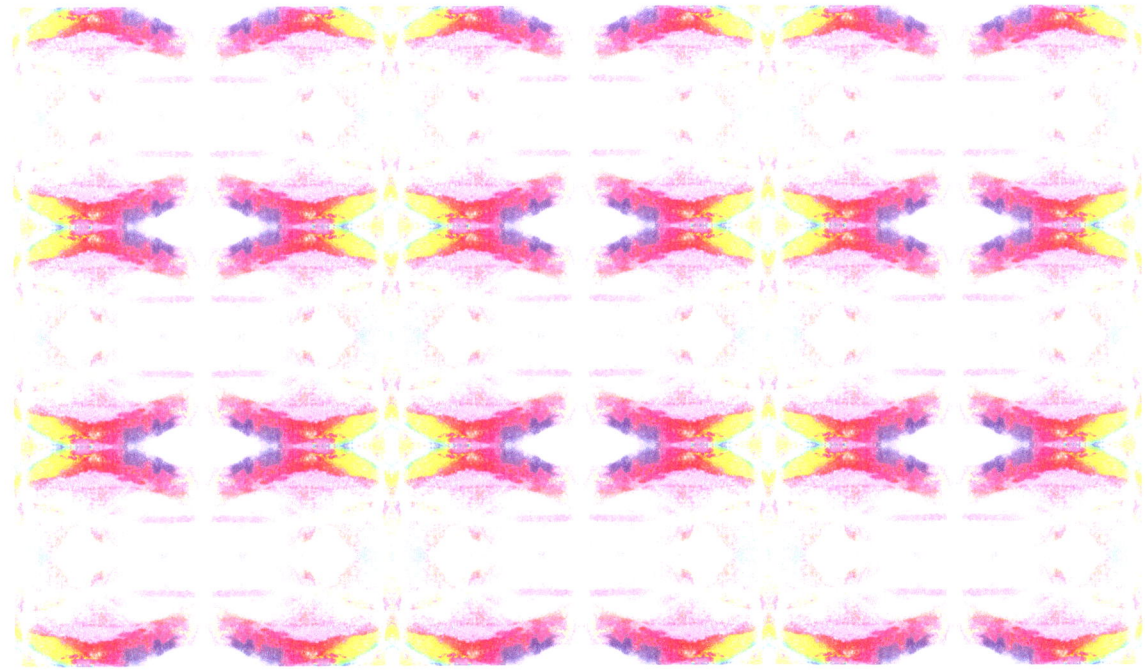

All Day

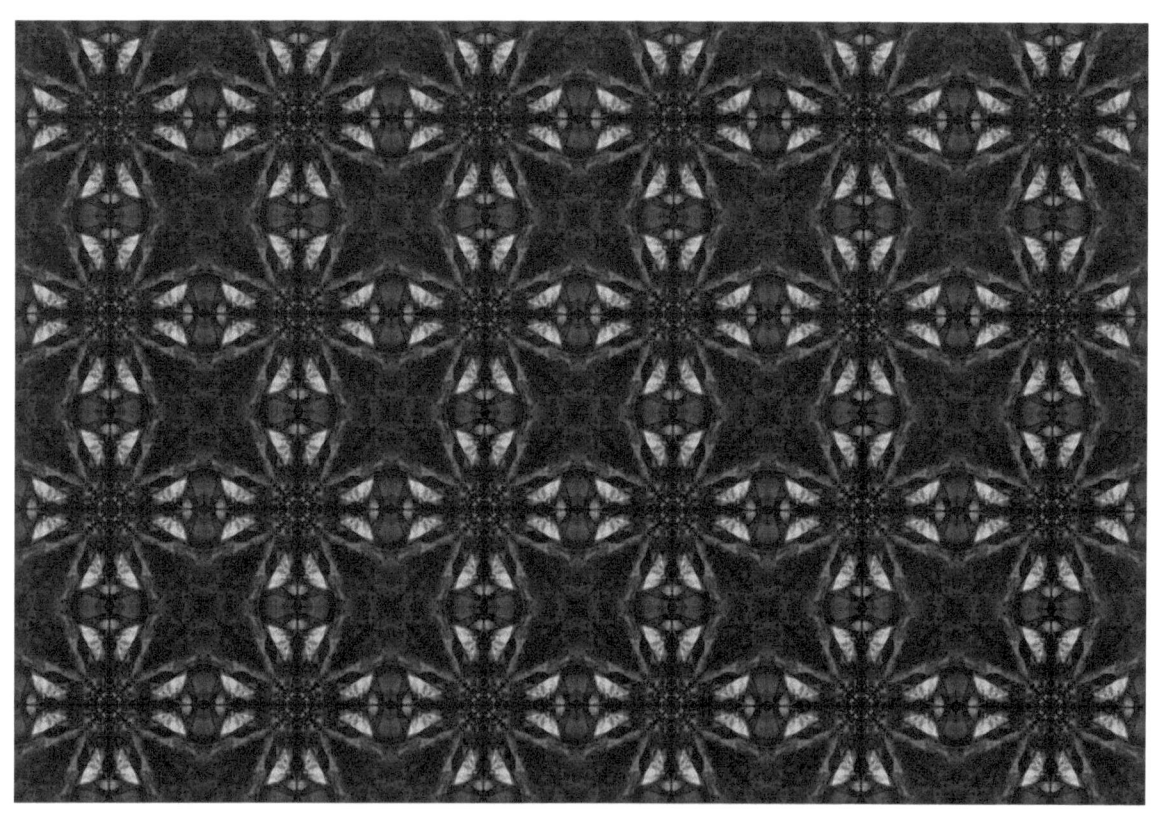

Alrighty Then

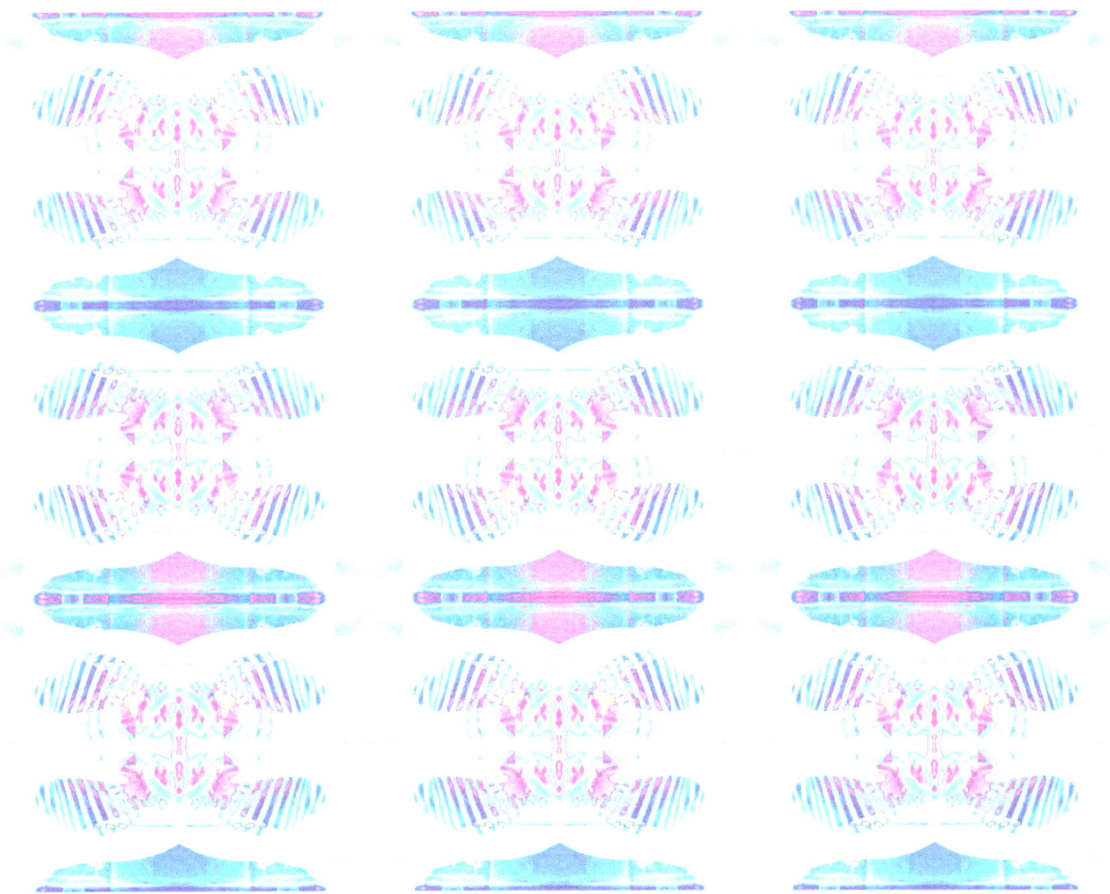

And Beaten

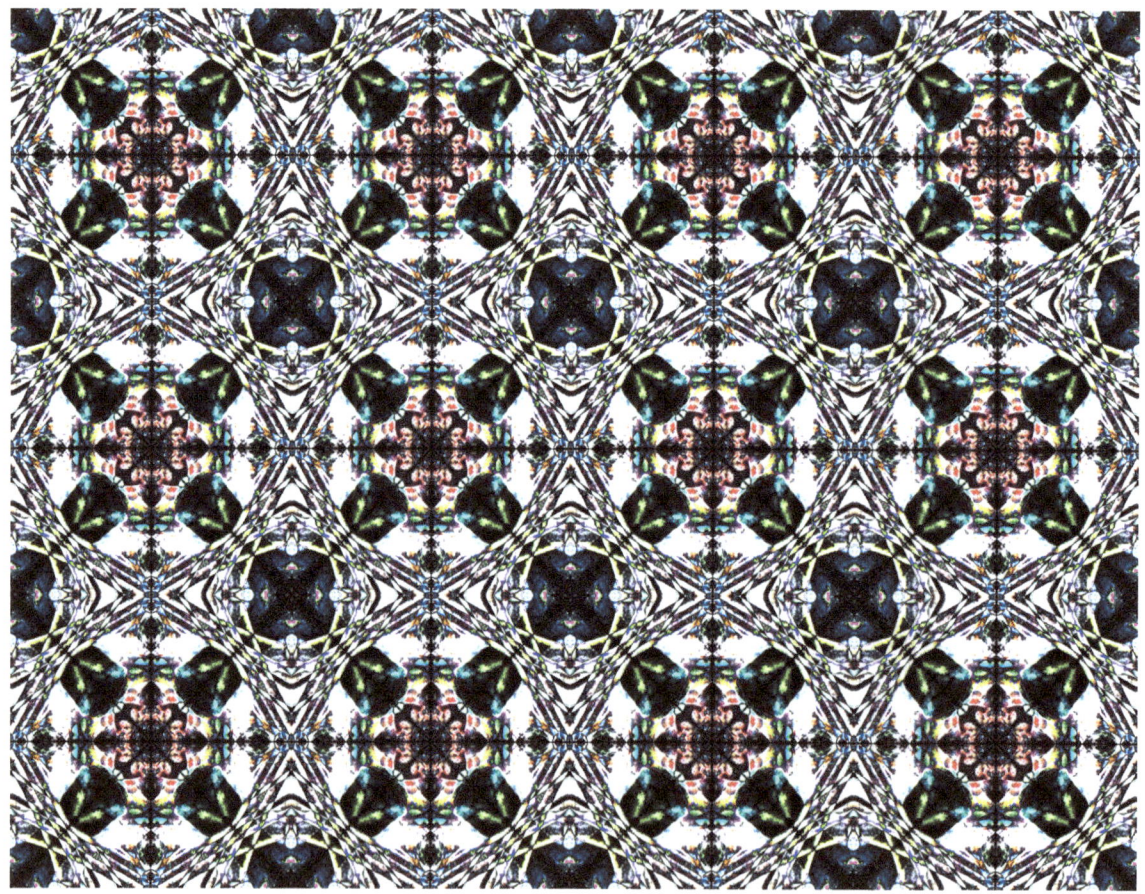

Back Today

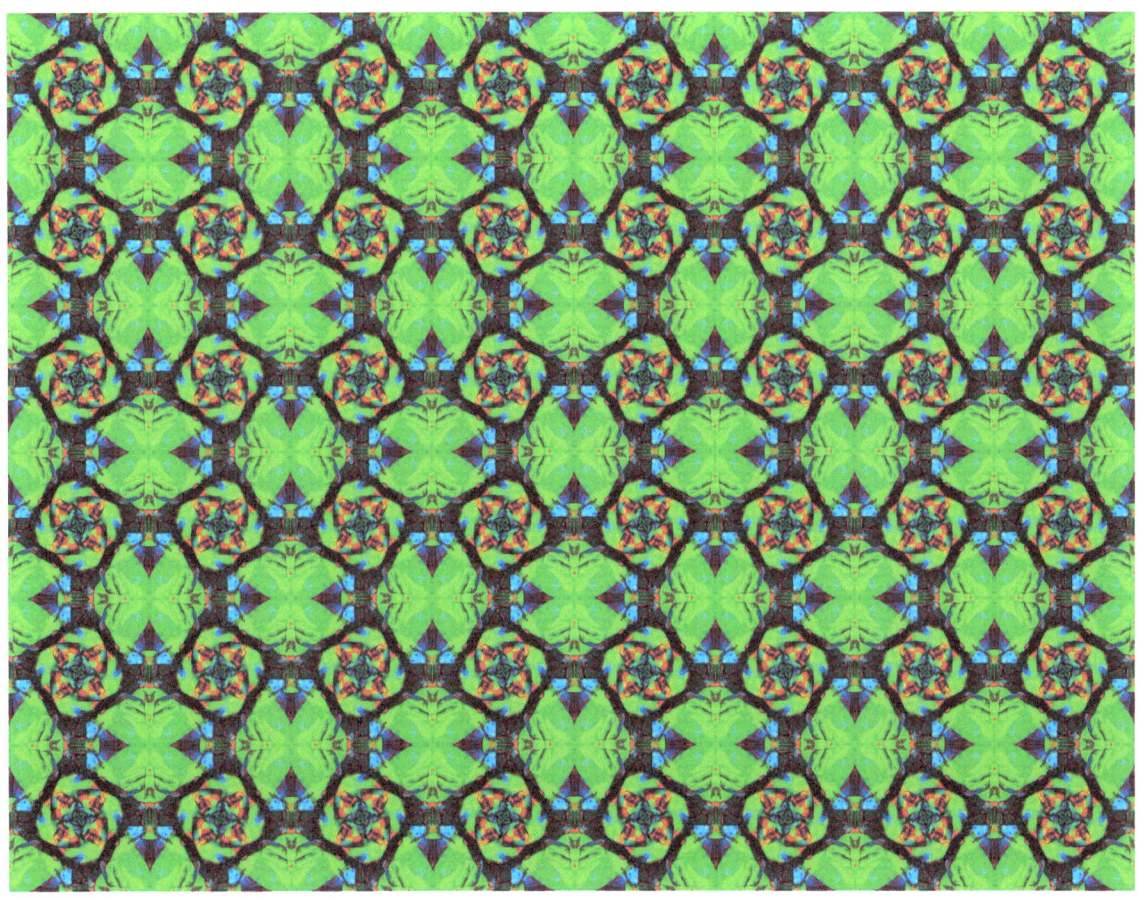

Being One

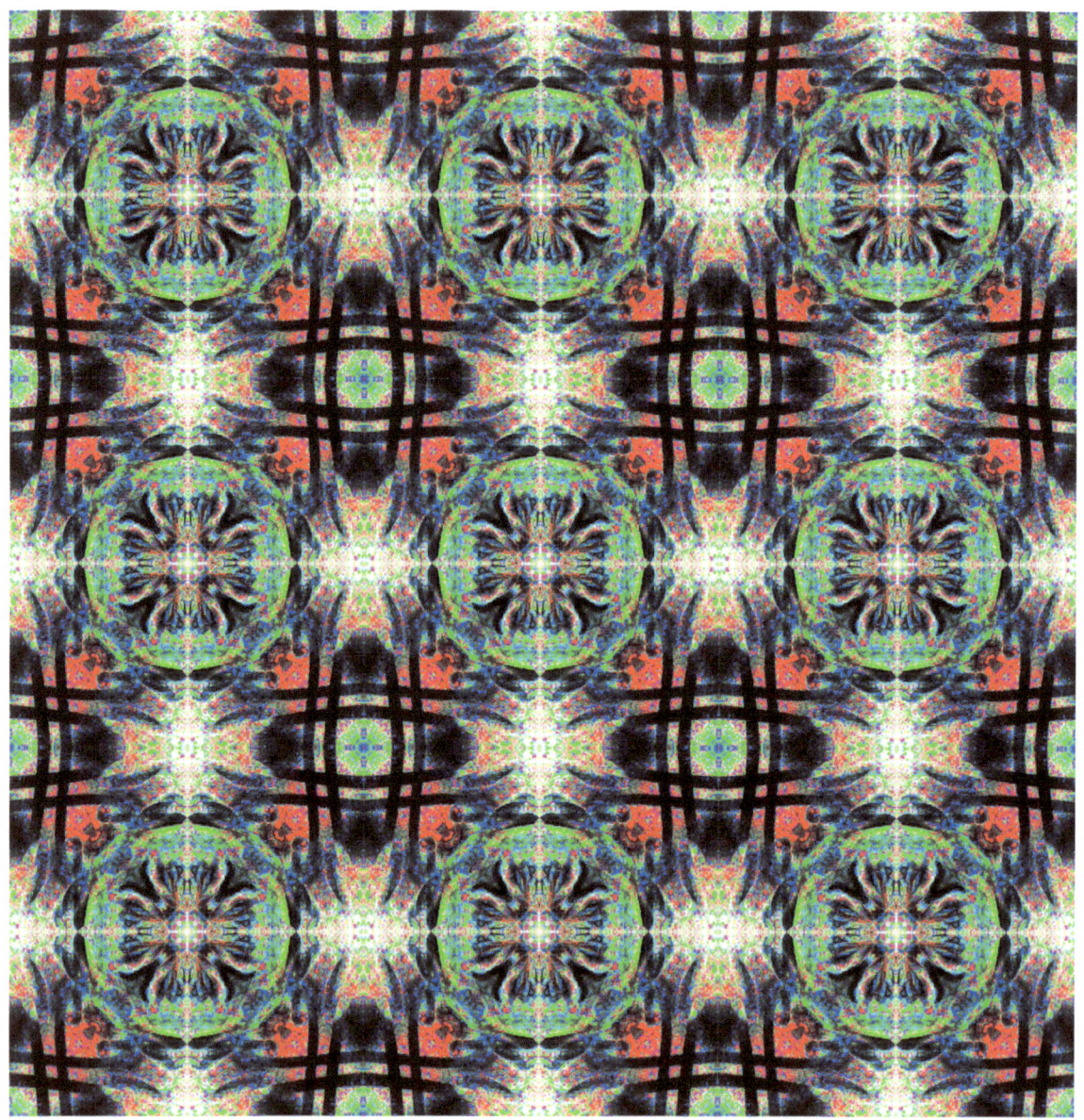

Being

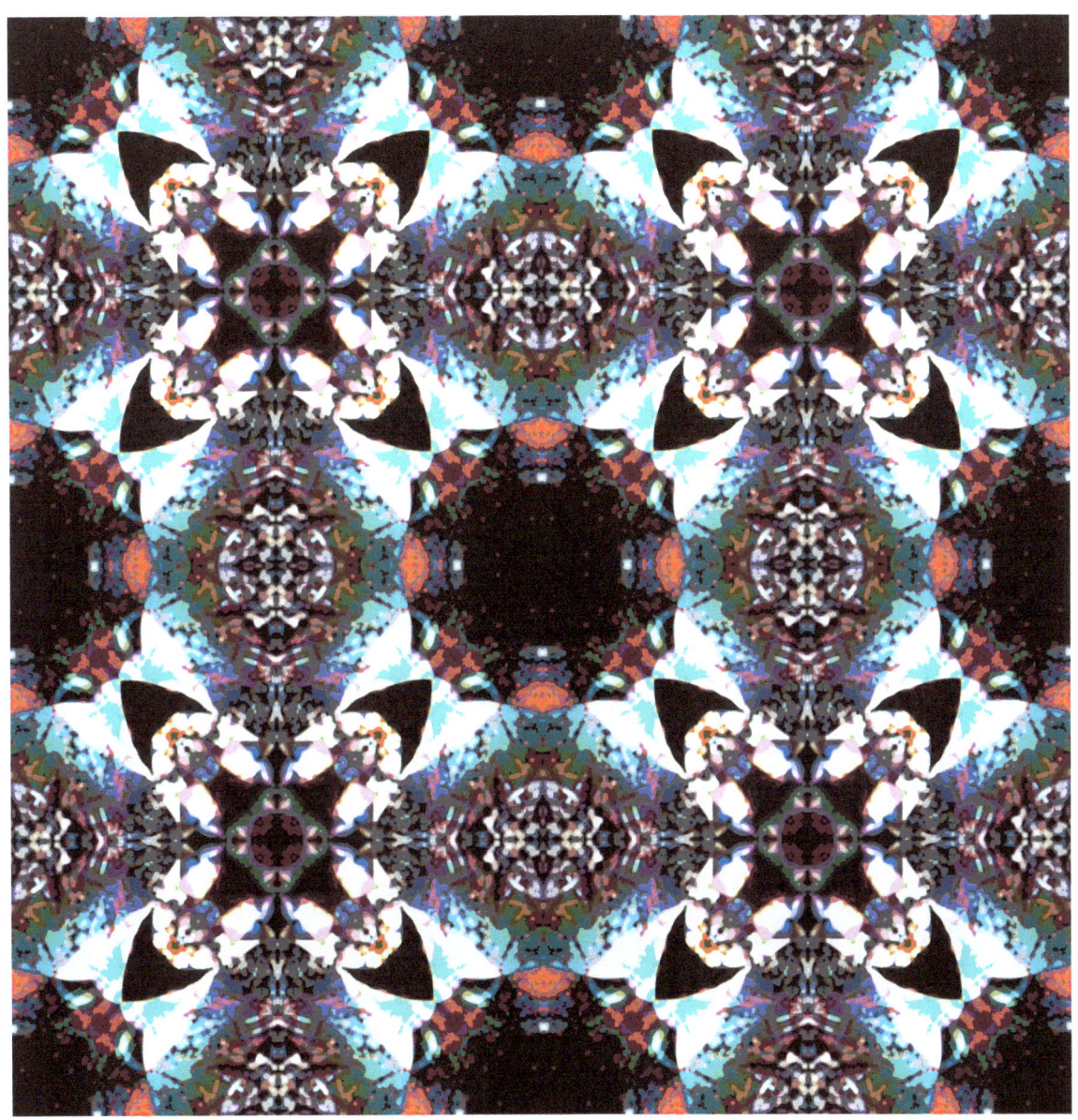

Being Stupid

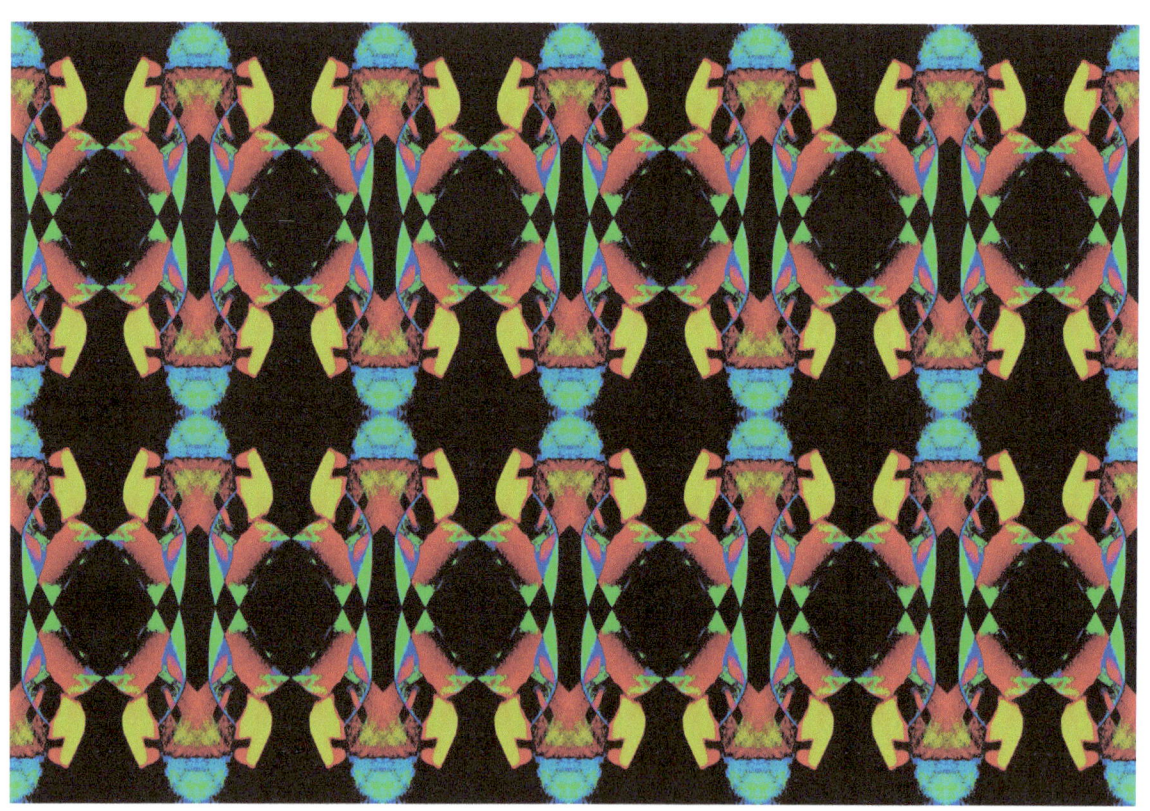

By Force

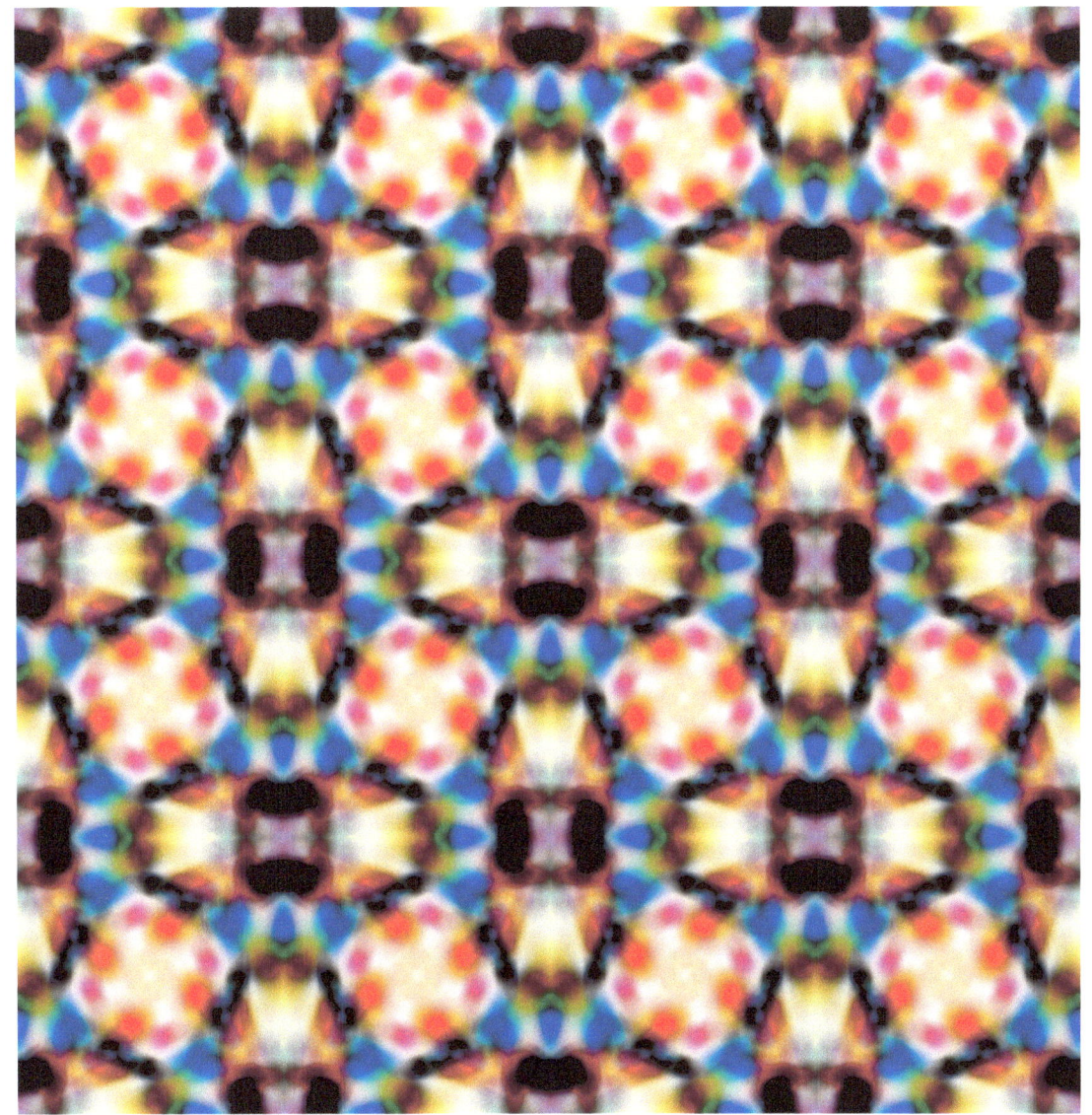

Can't Stop

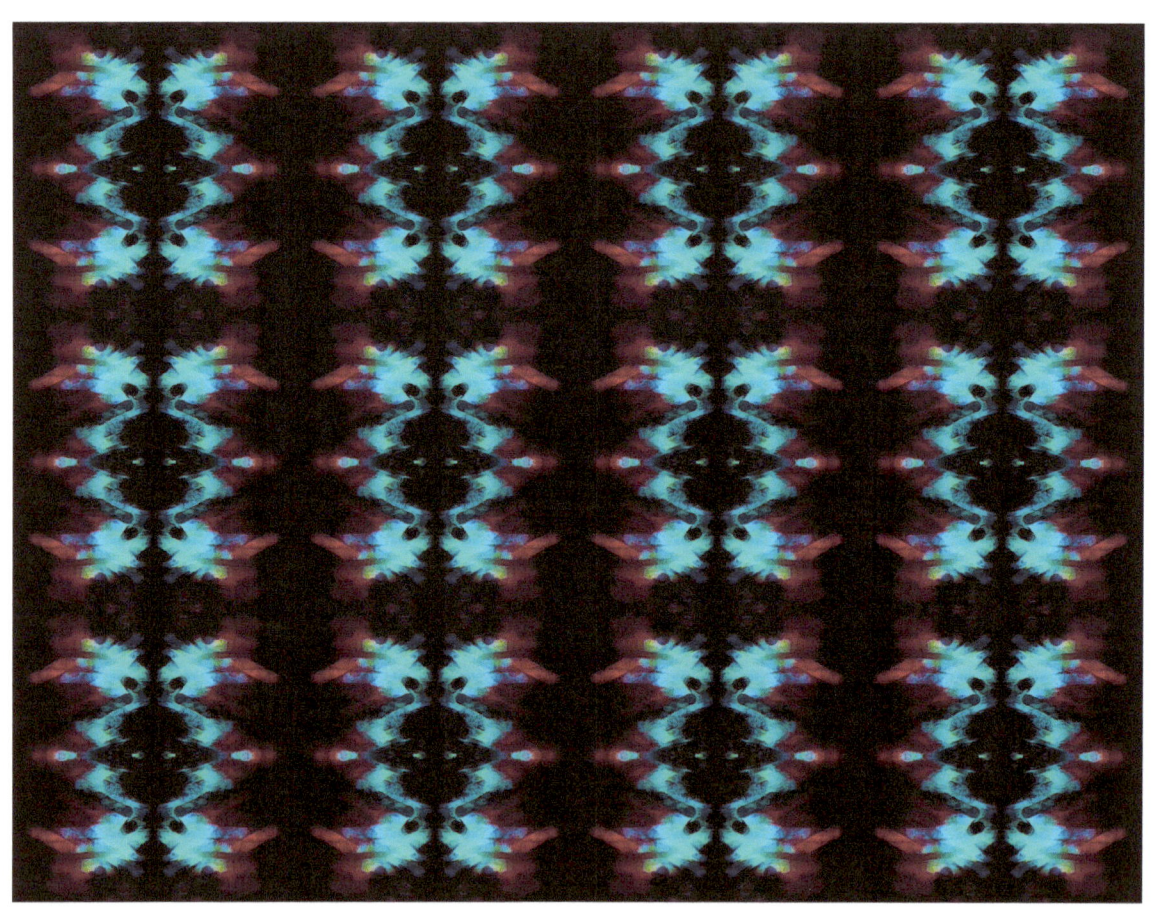

Catch Me

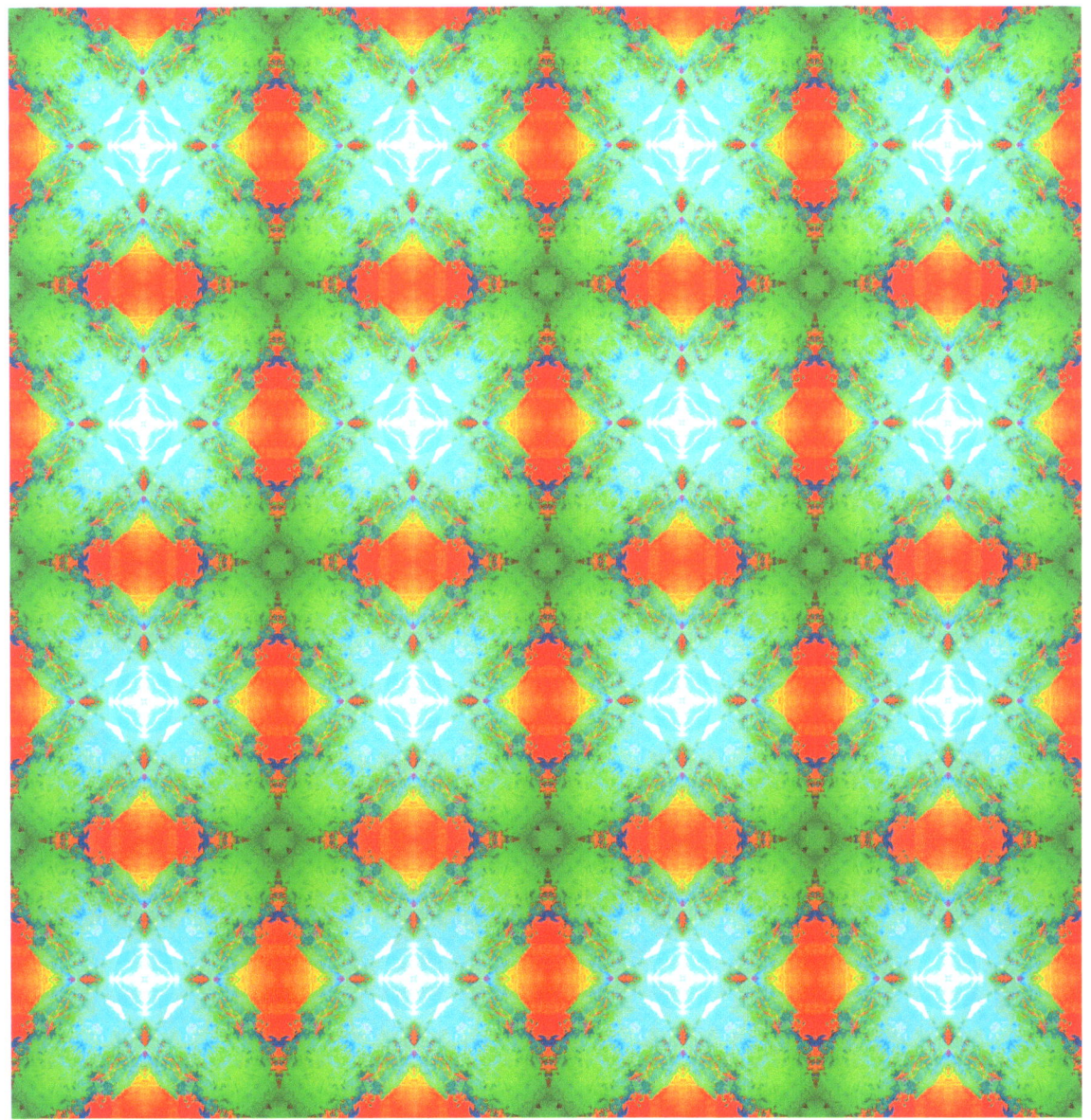

Could Happen

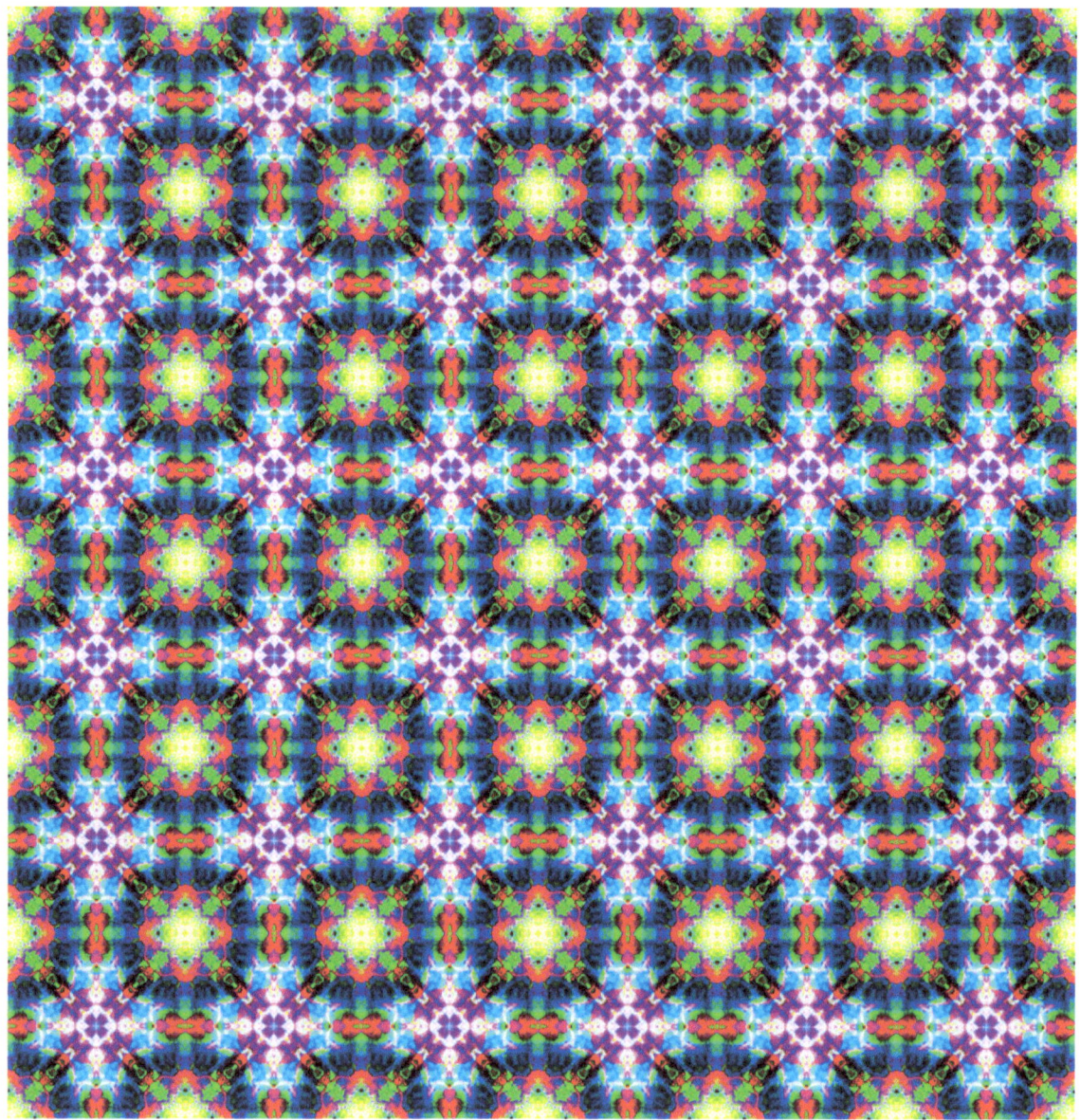

Detached

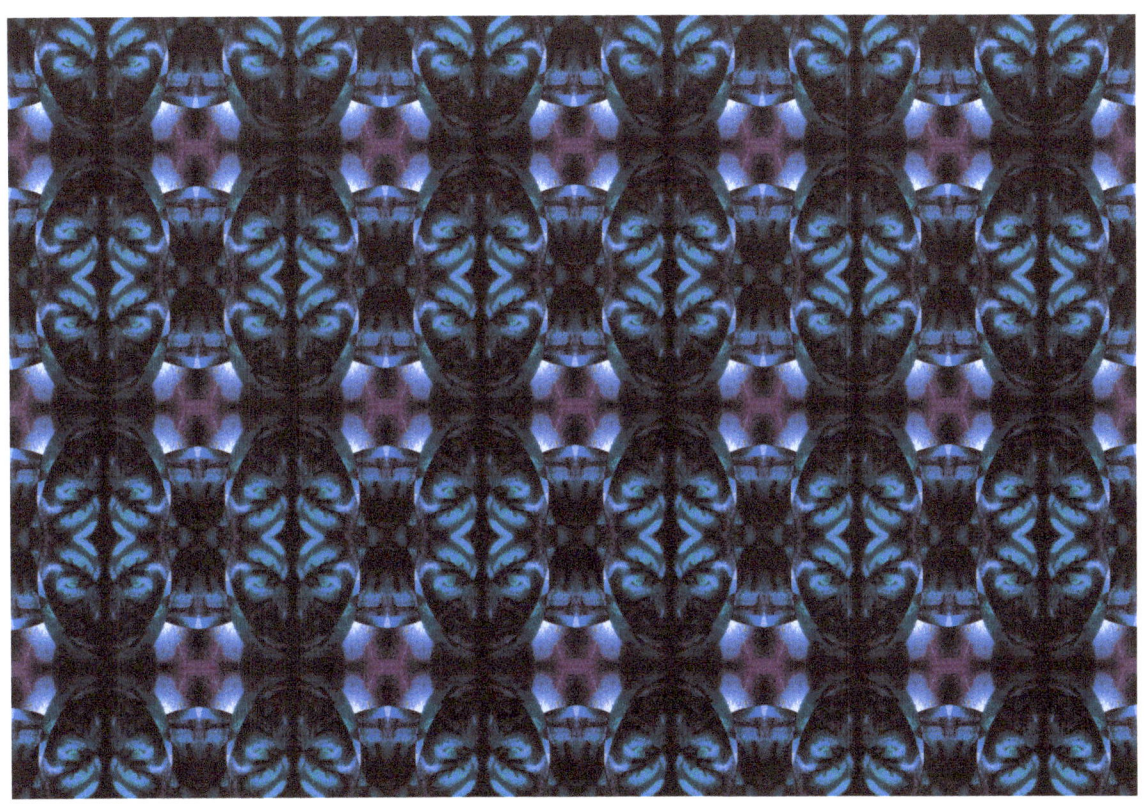

Every Free Moment

Good Idea

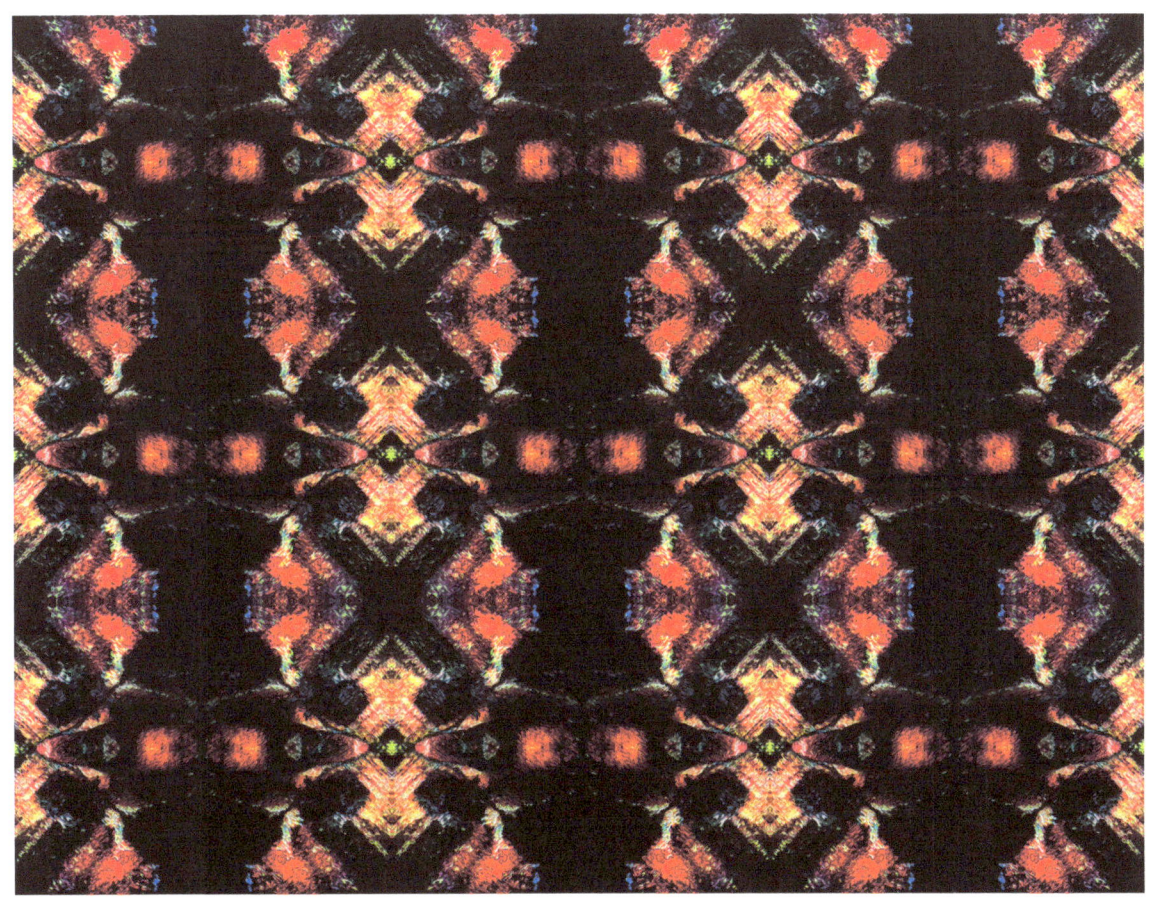

Got Done

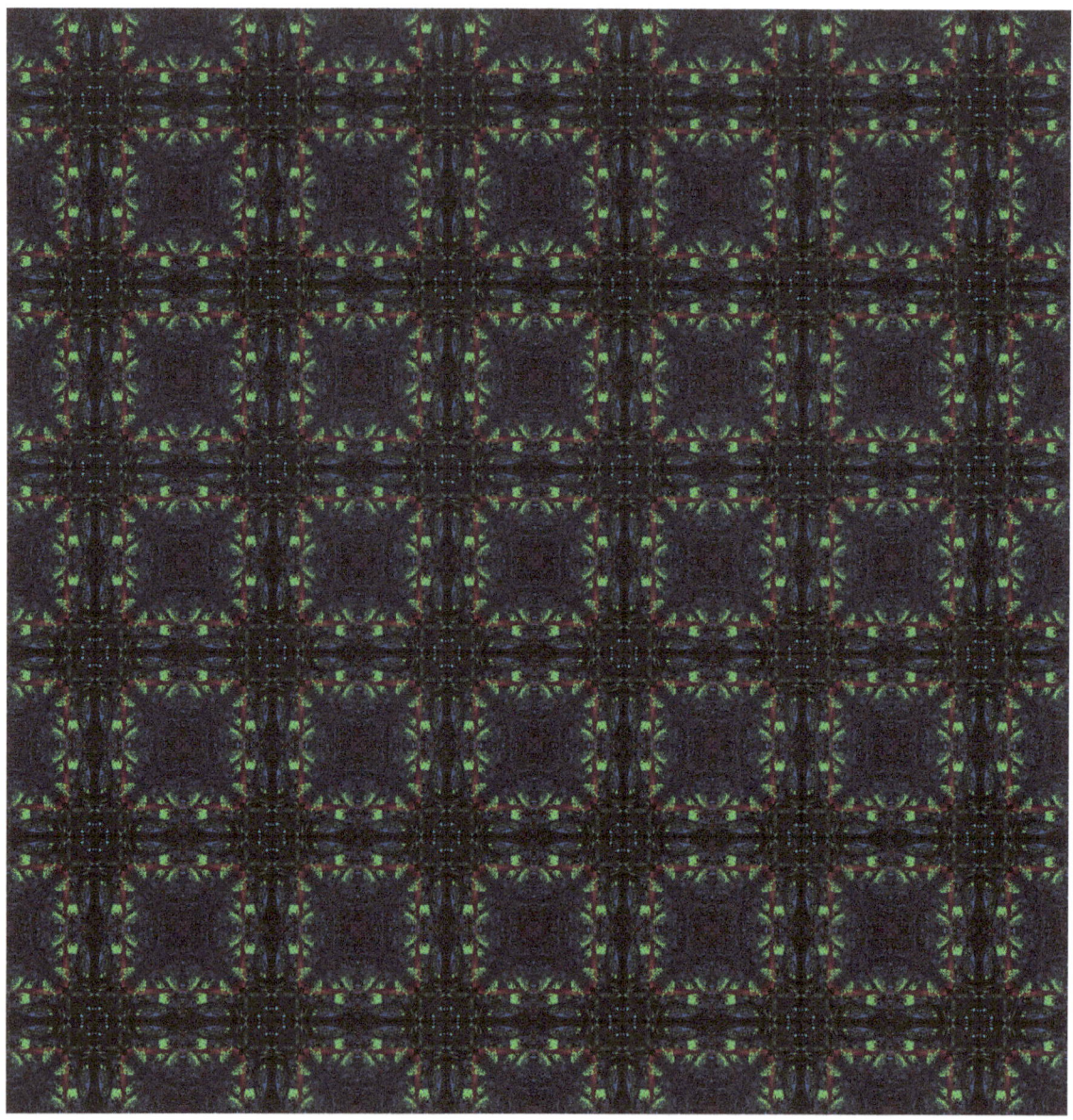

Hit You

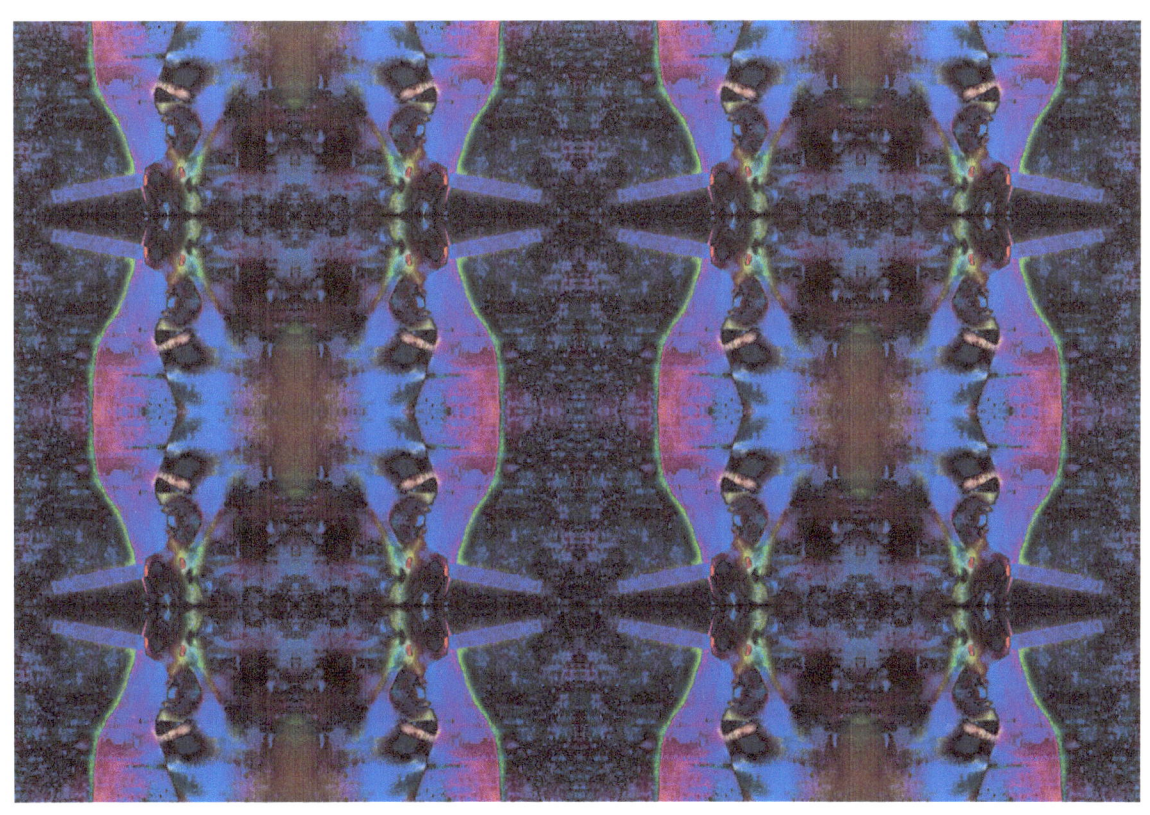

I Think I'd Die

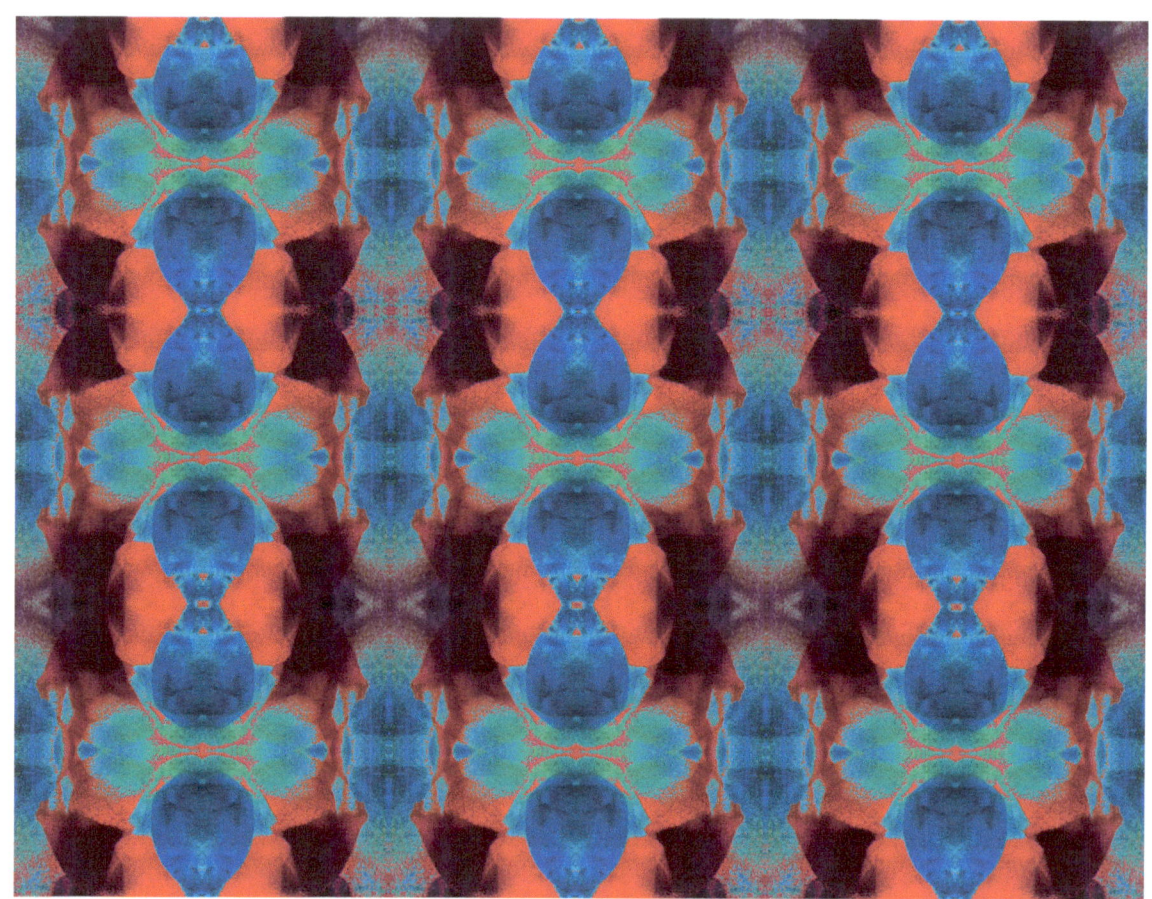

Just A Bonus

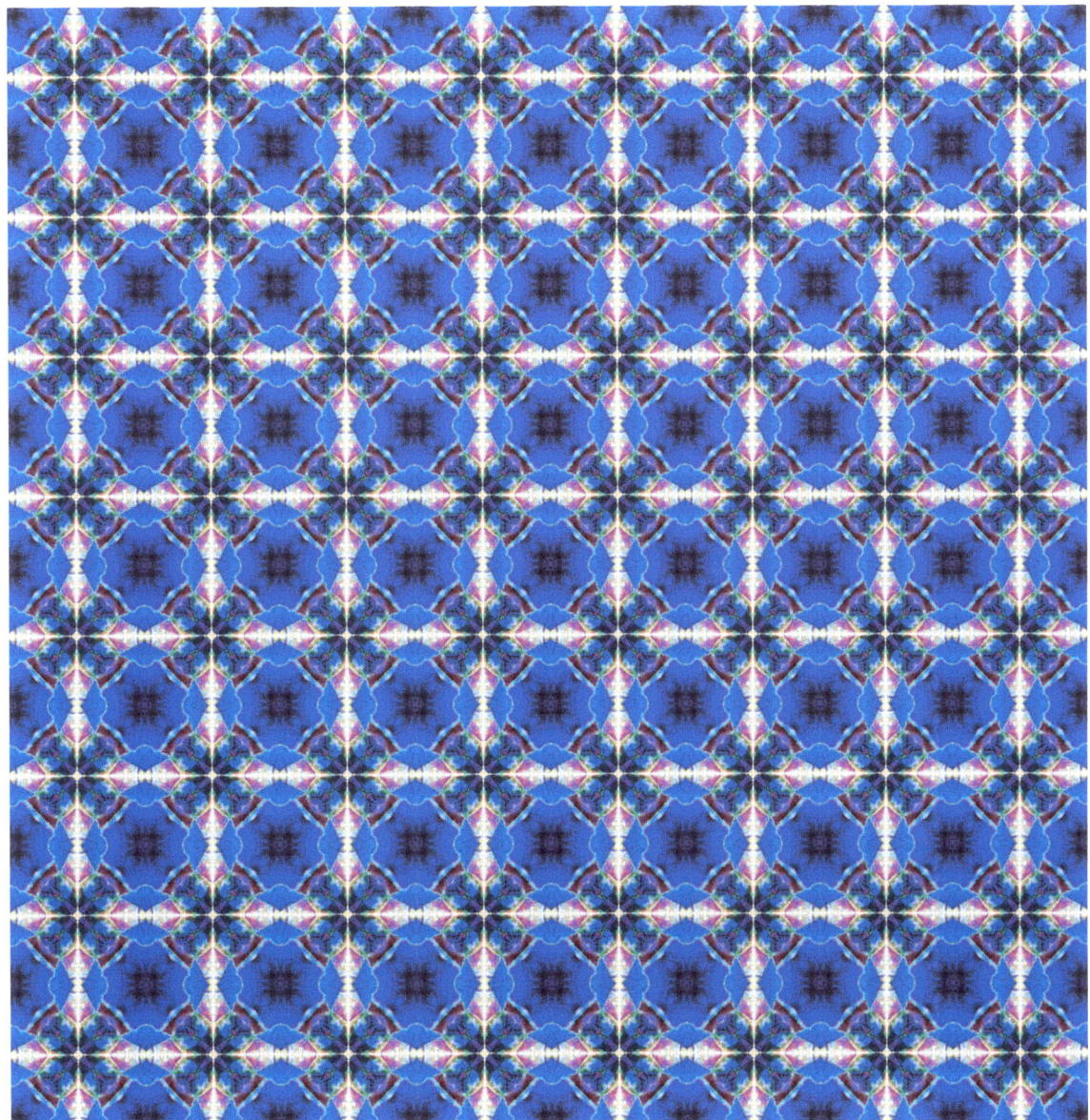

Keeps Shaking

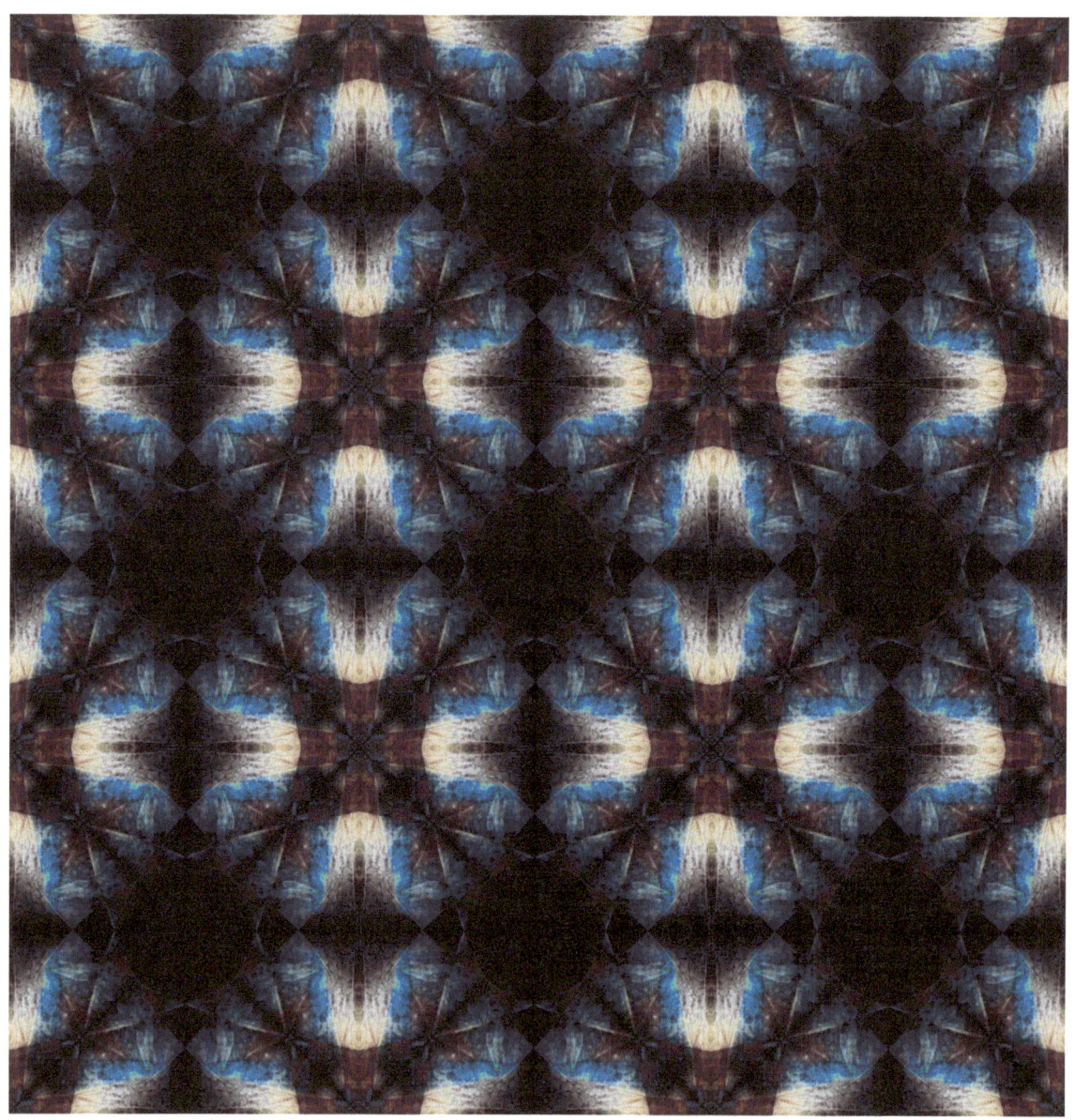

Last Time

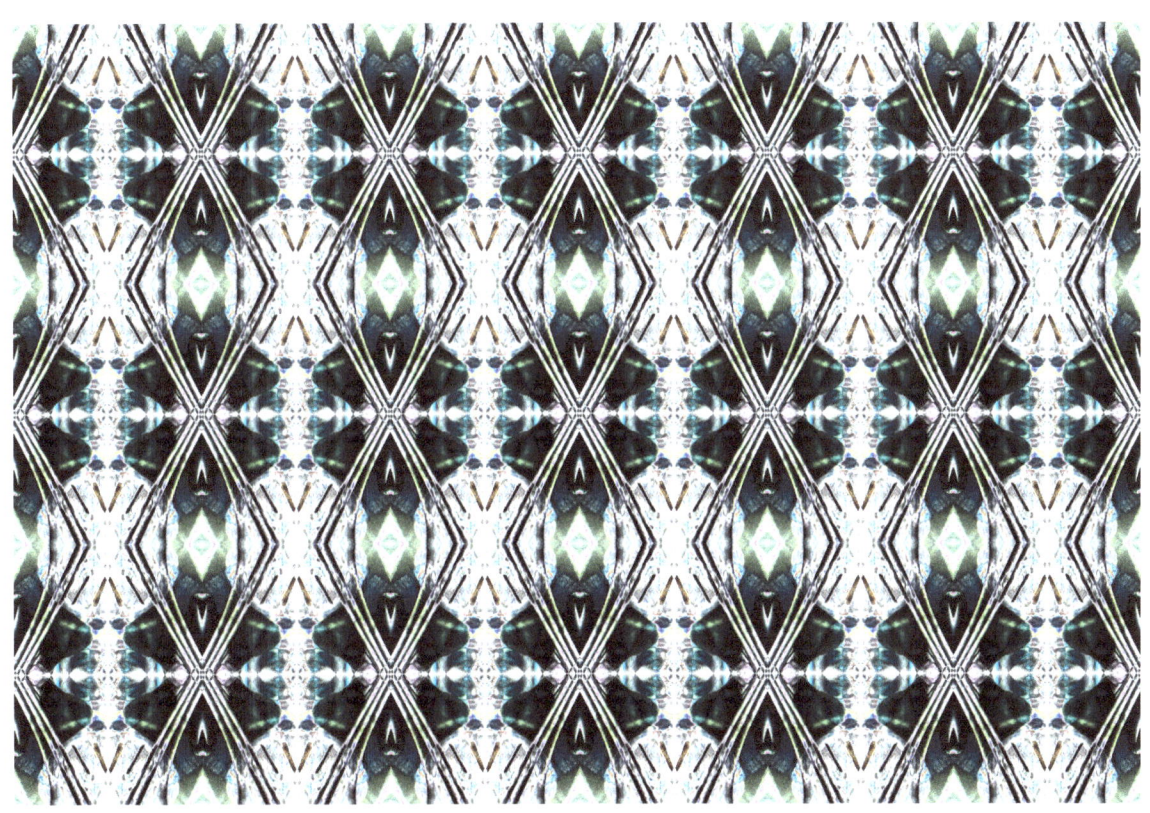

Lasts Longer

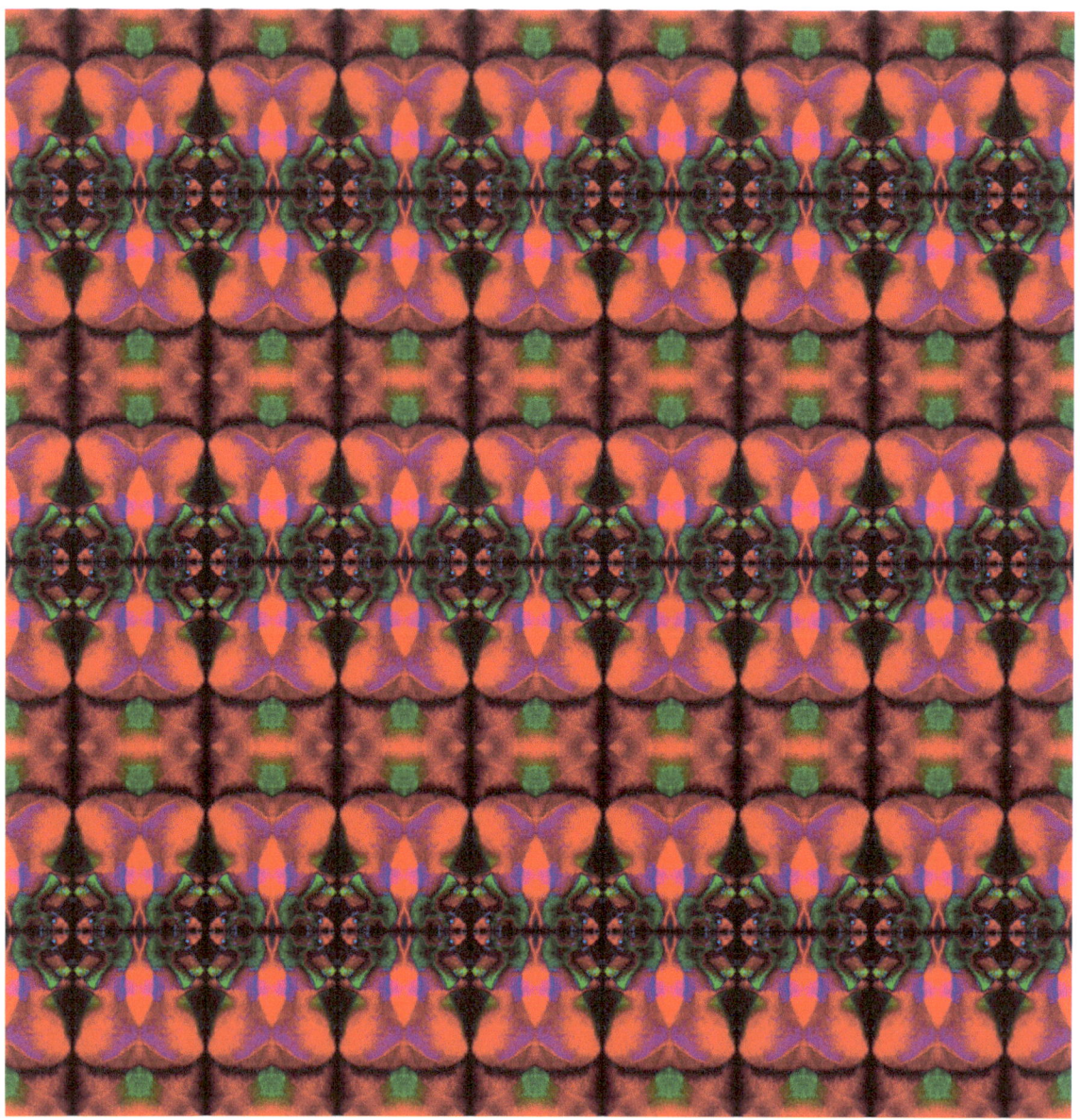

Long Day

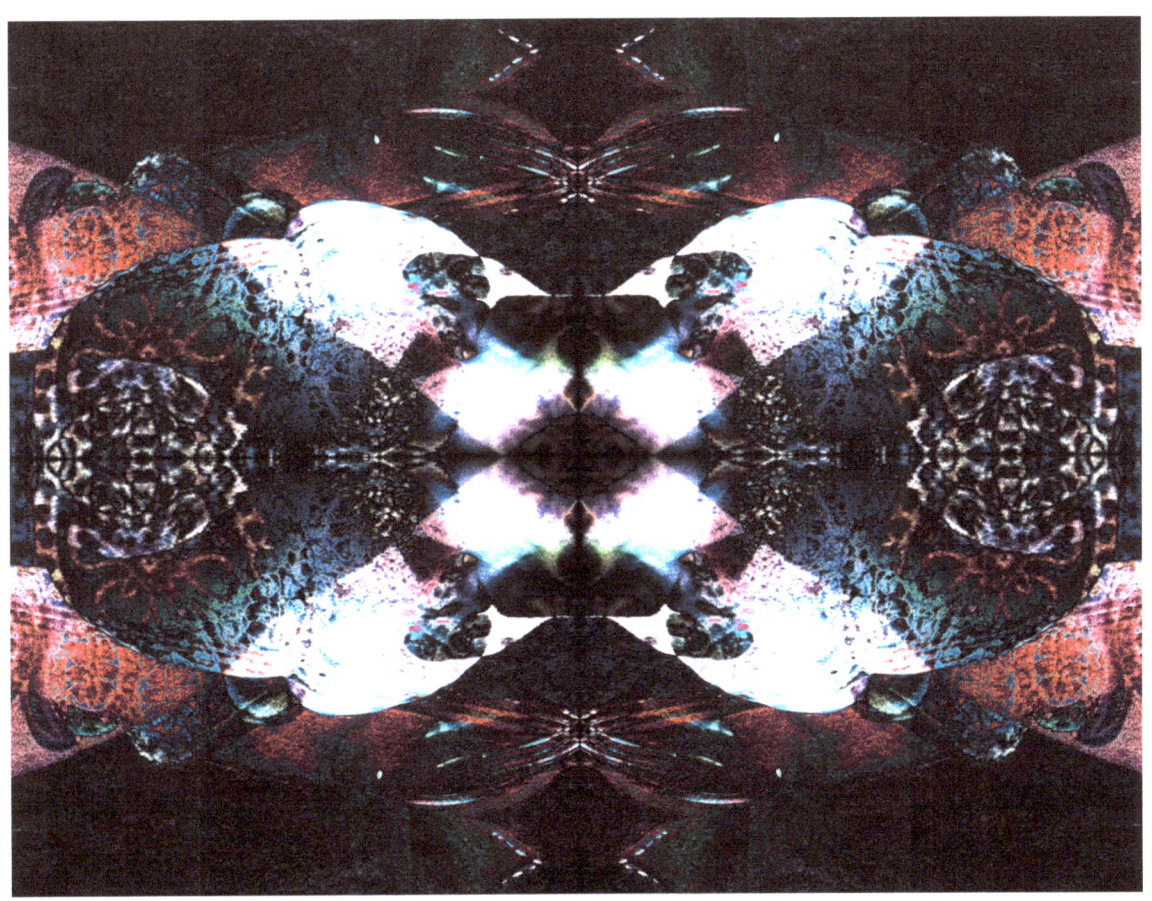

Look Forward

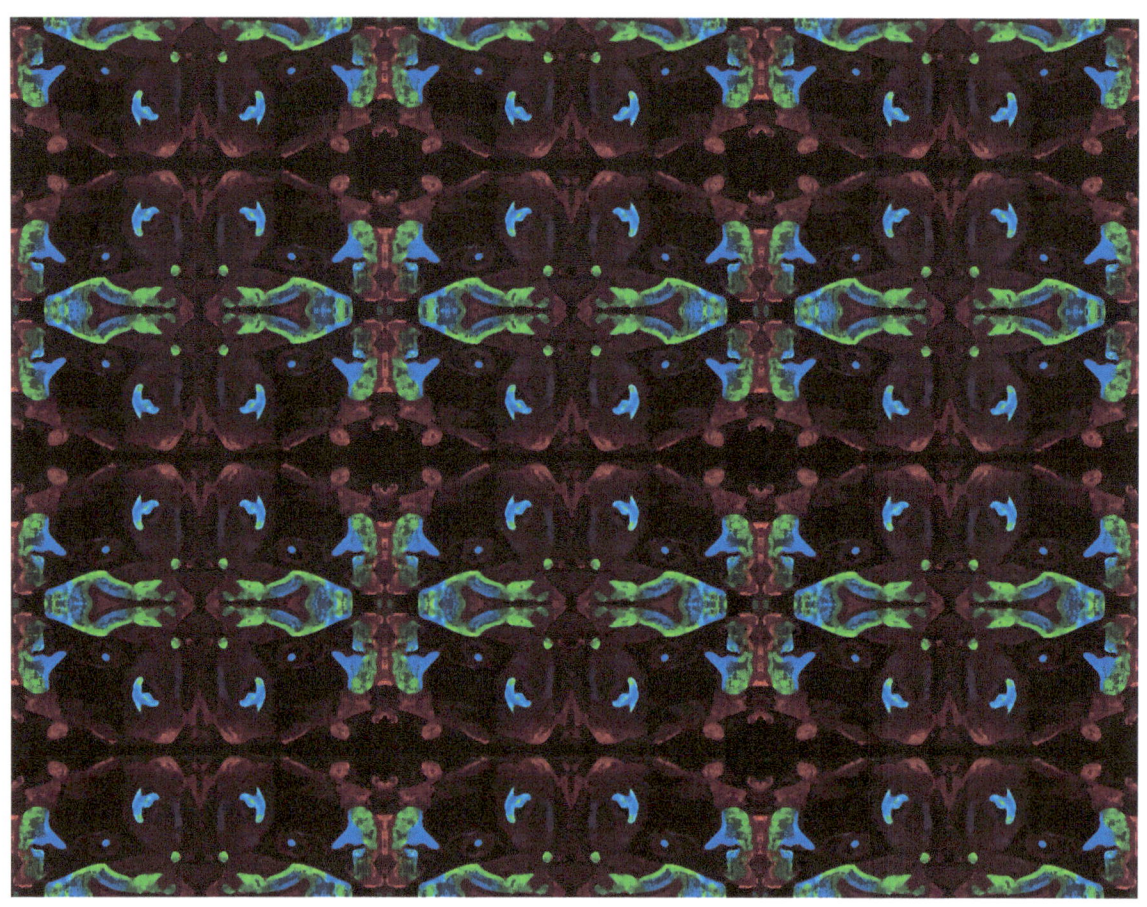

Never Ask

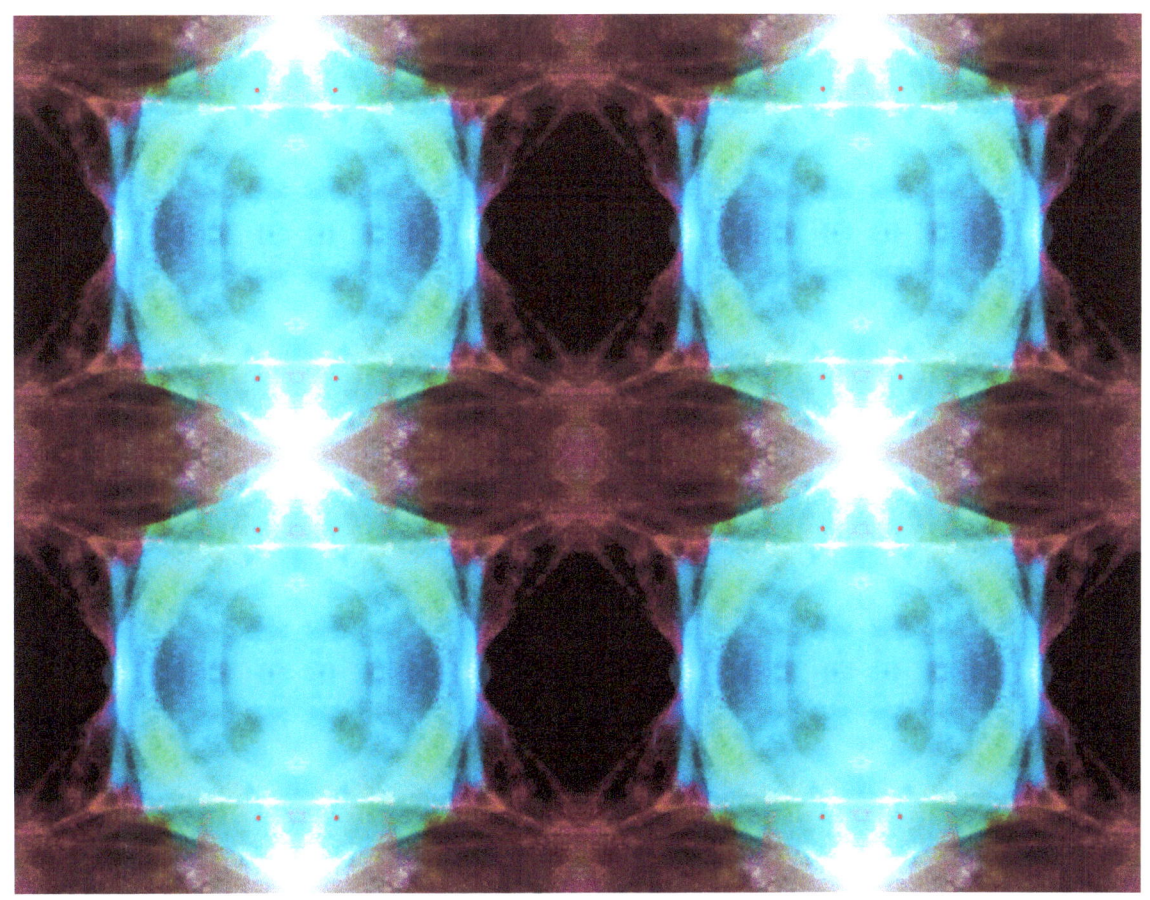

On Purpose

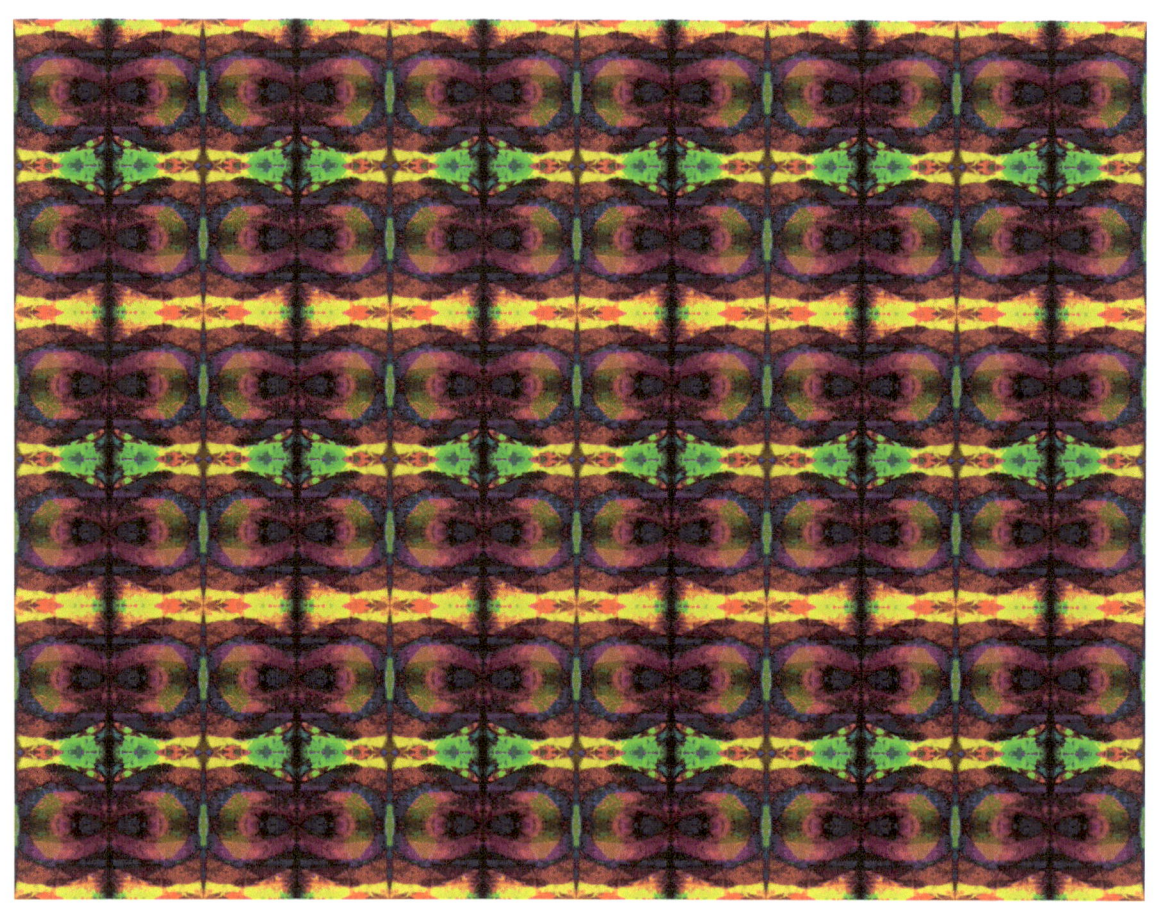

Only Care

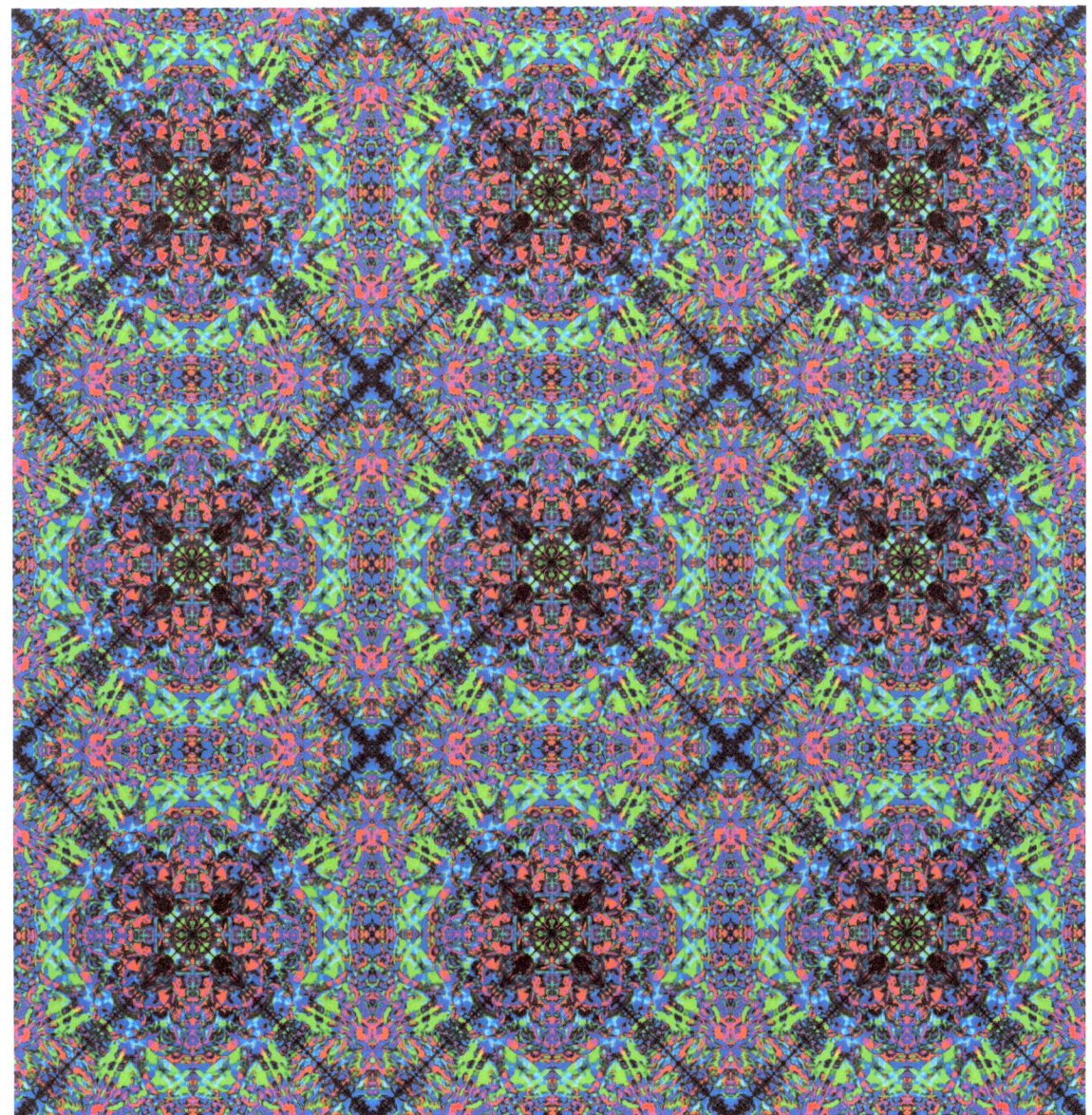

Right Now

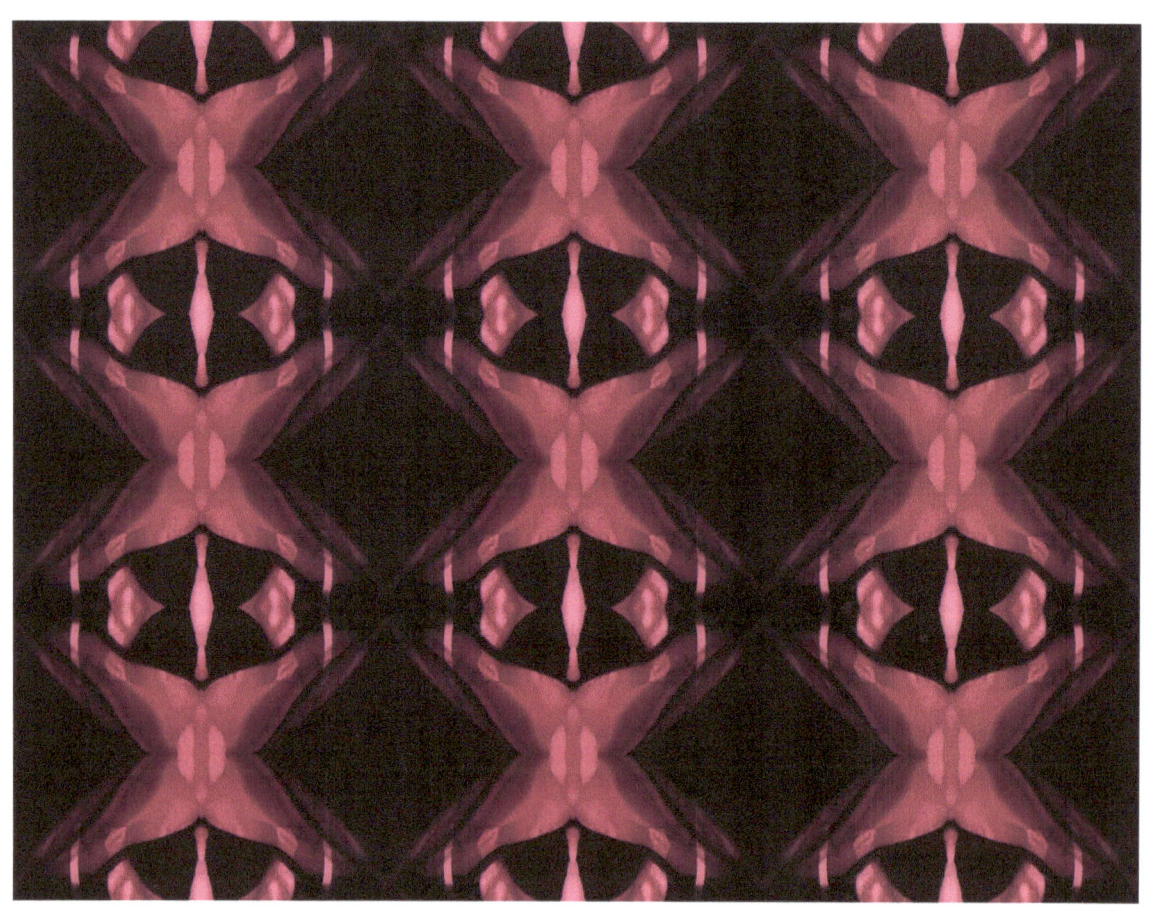

Say That

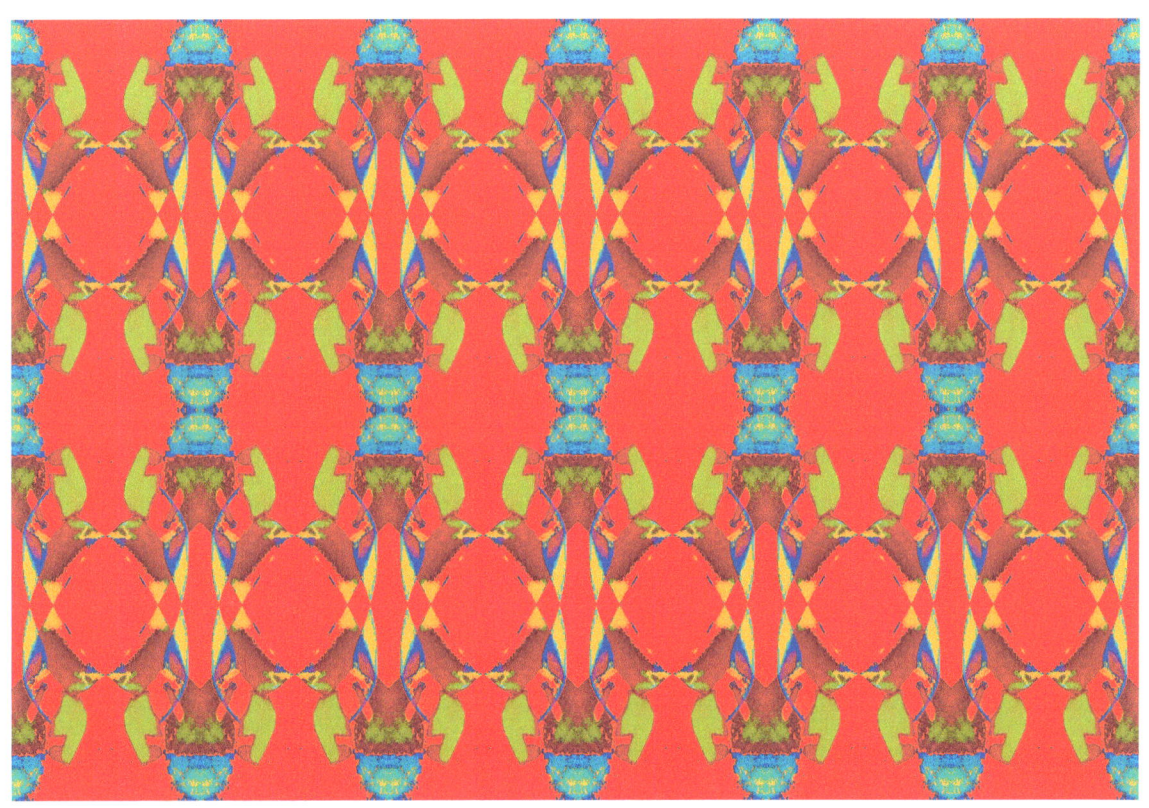

Shut Up

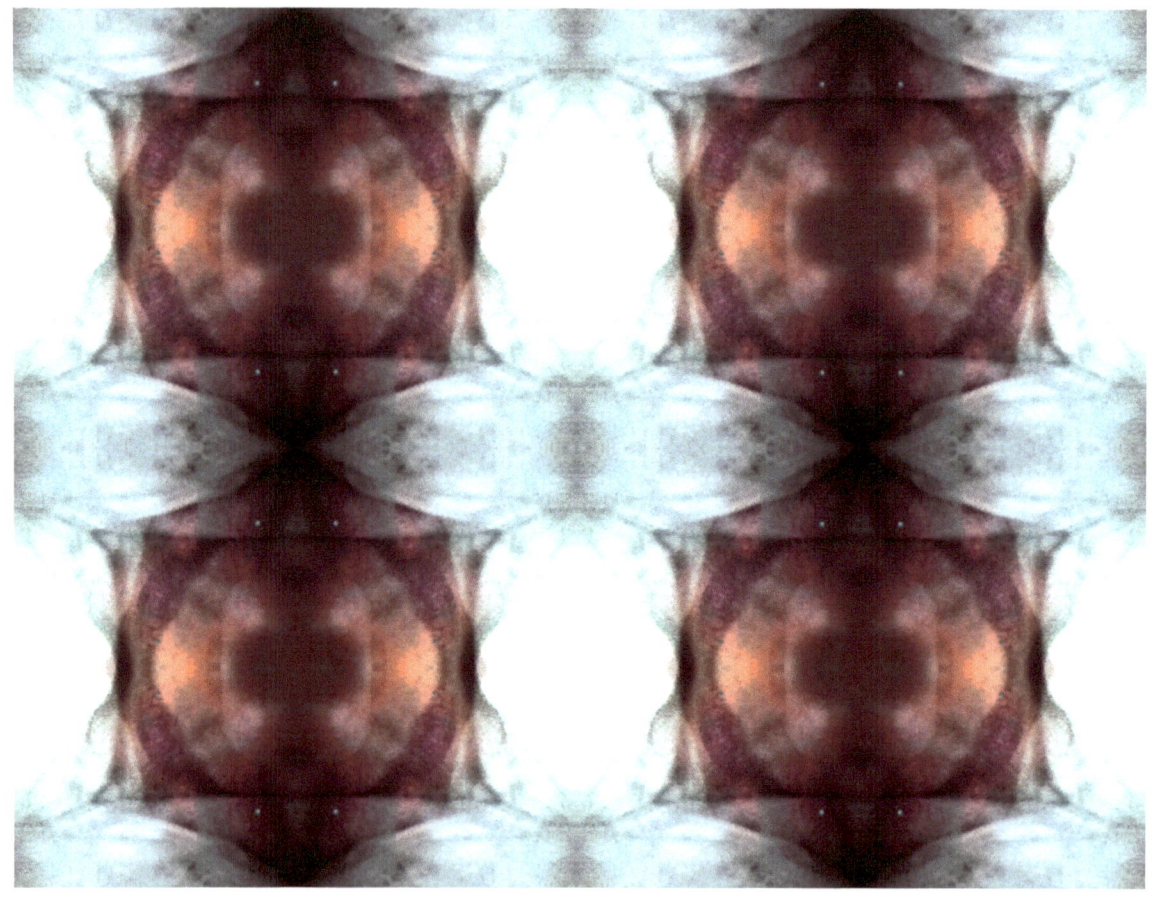

Still Waiting

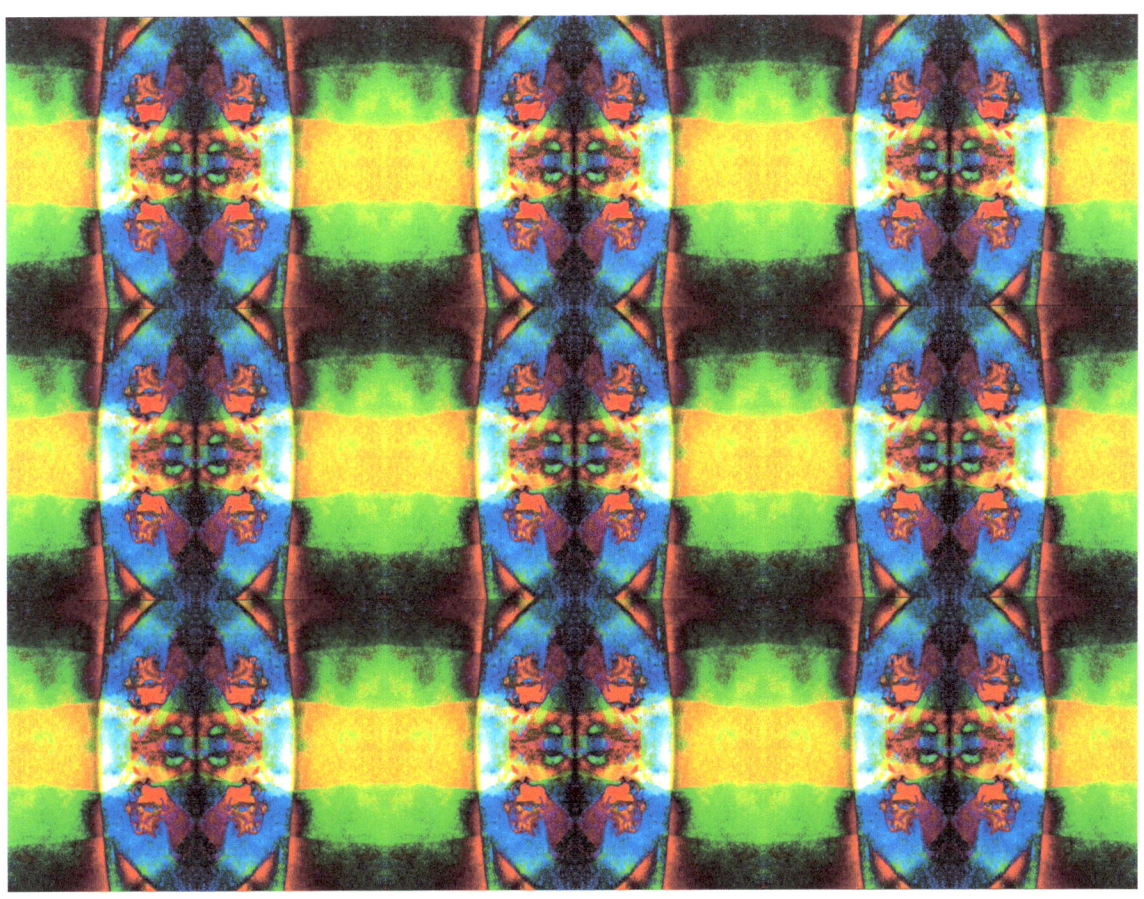

Taking Everything

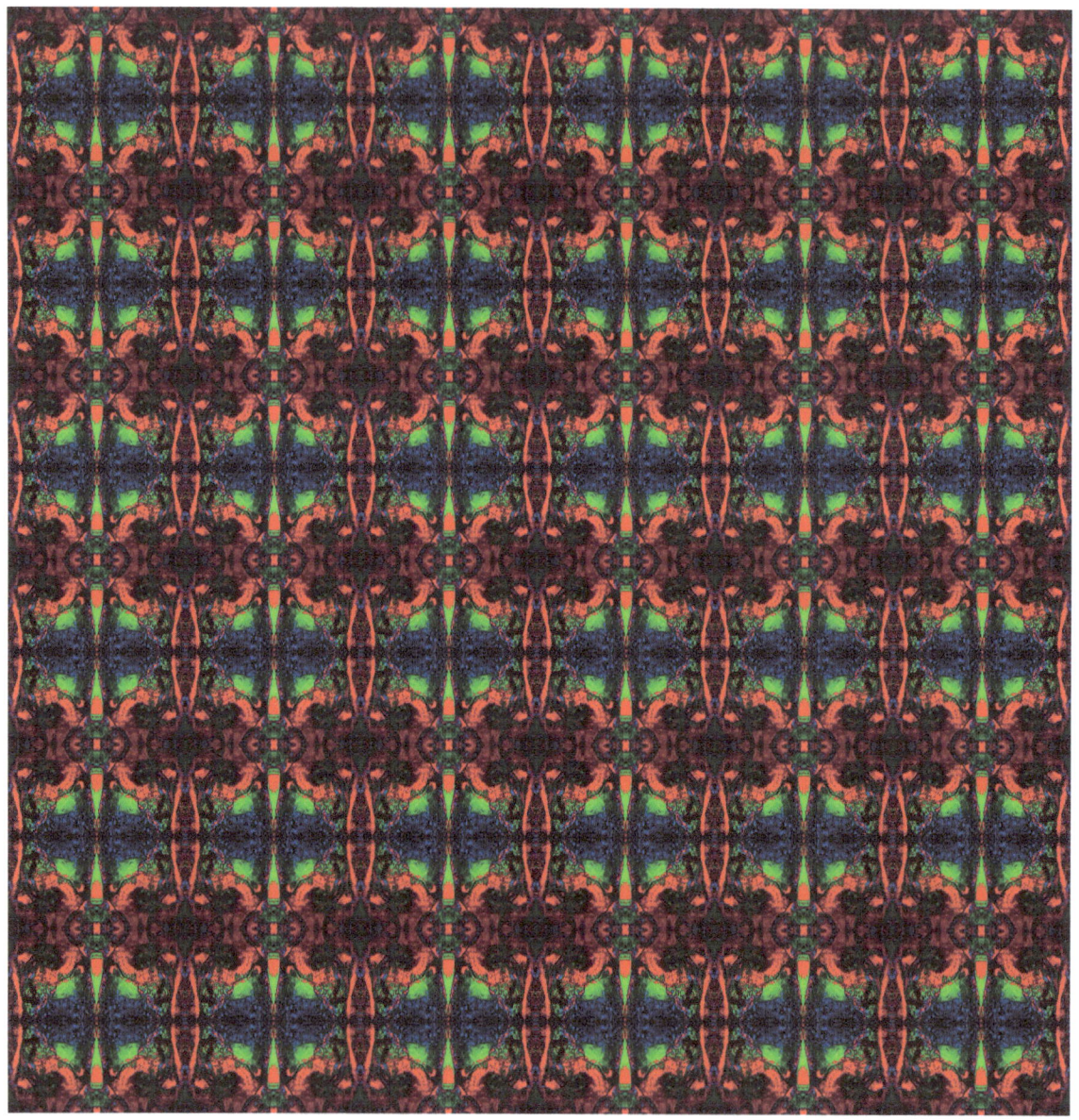

Terrifies Me

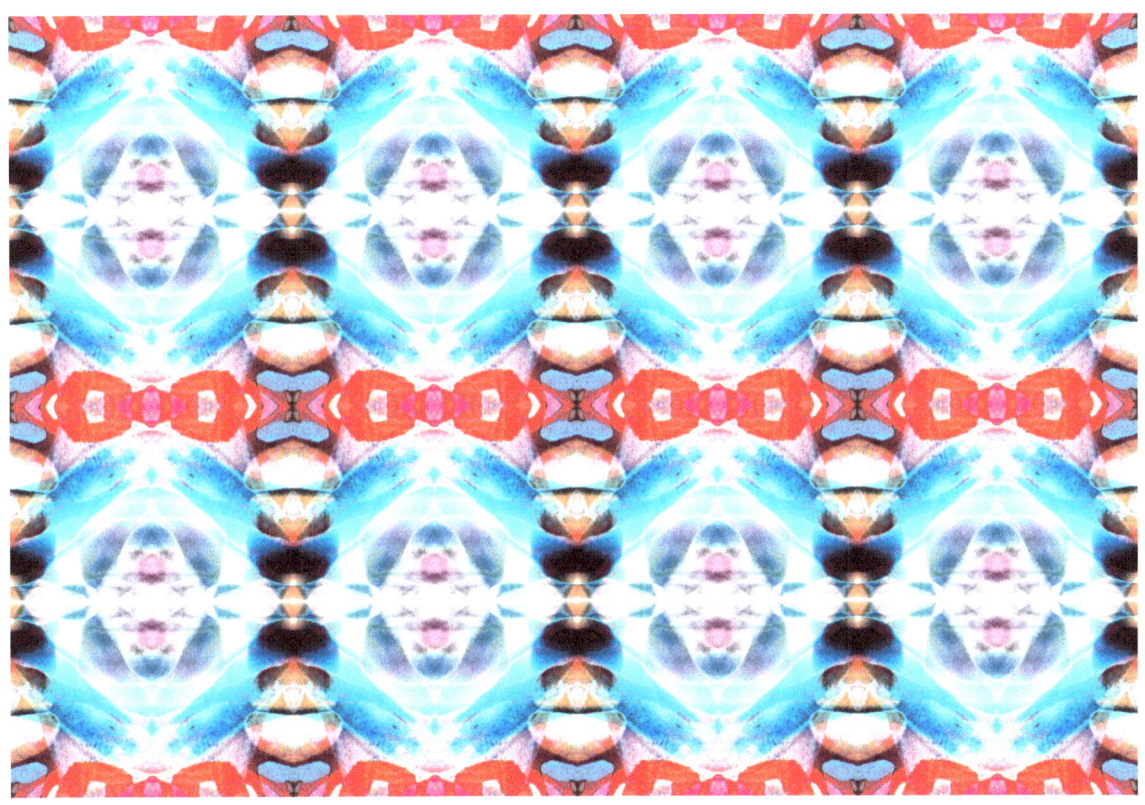

That Was

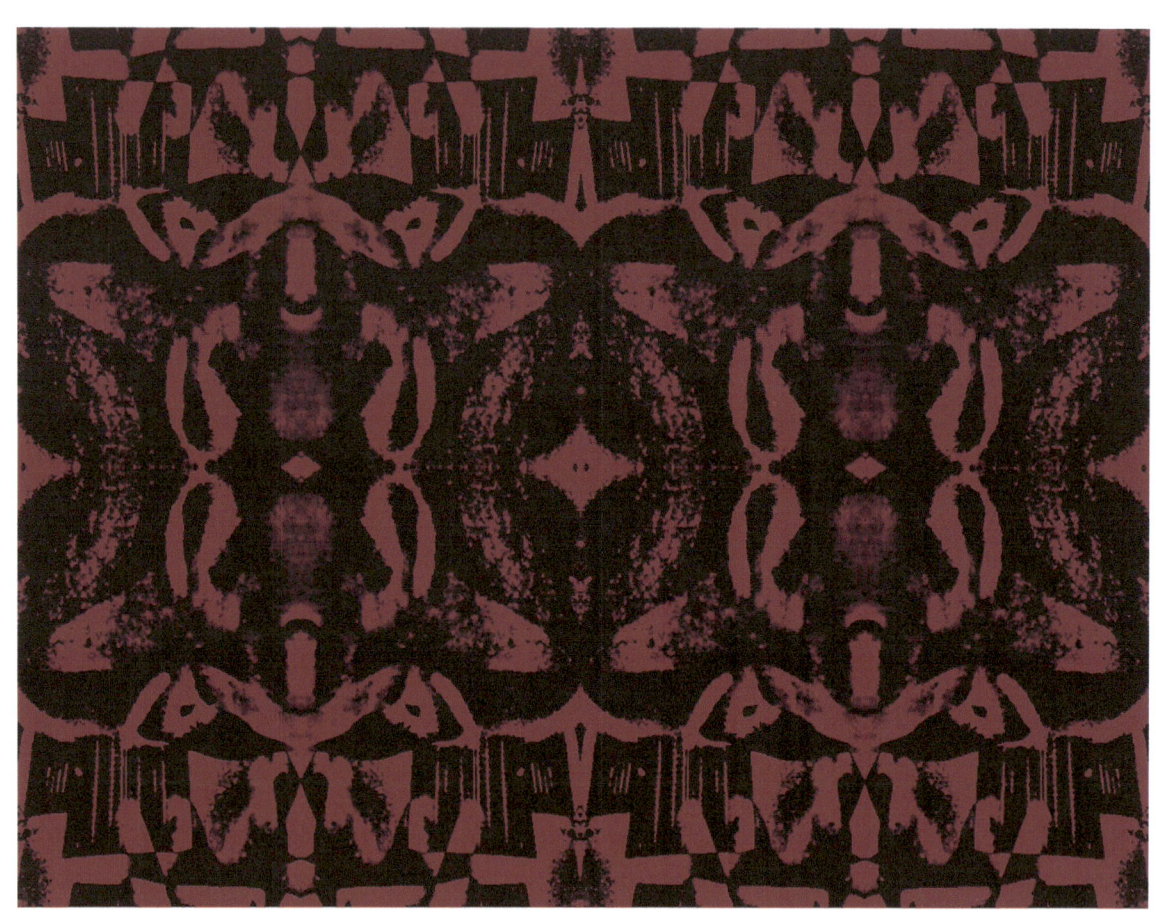

That's What You Get

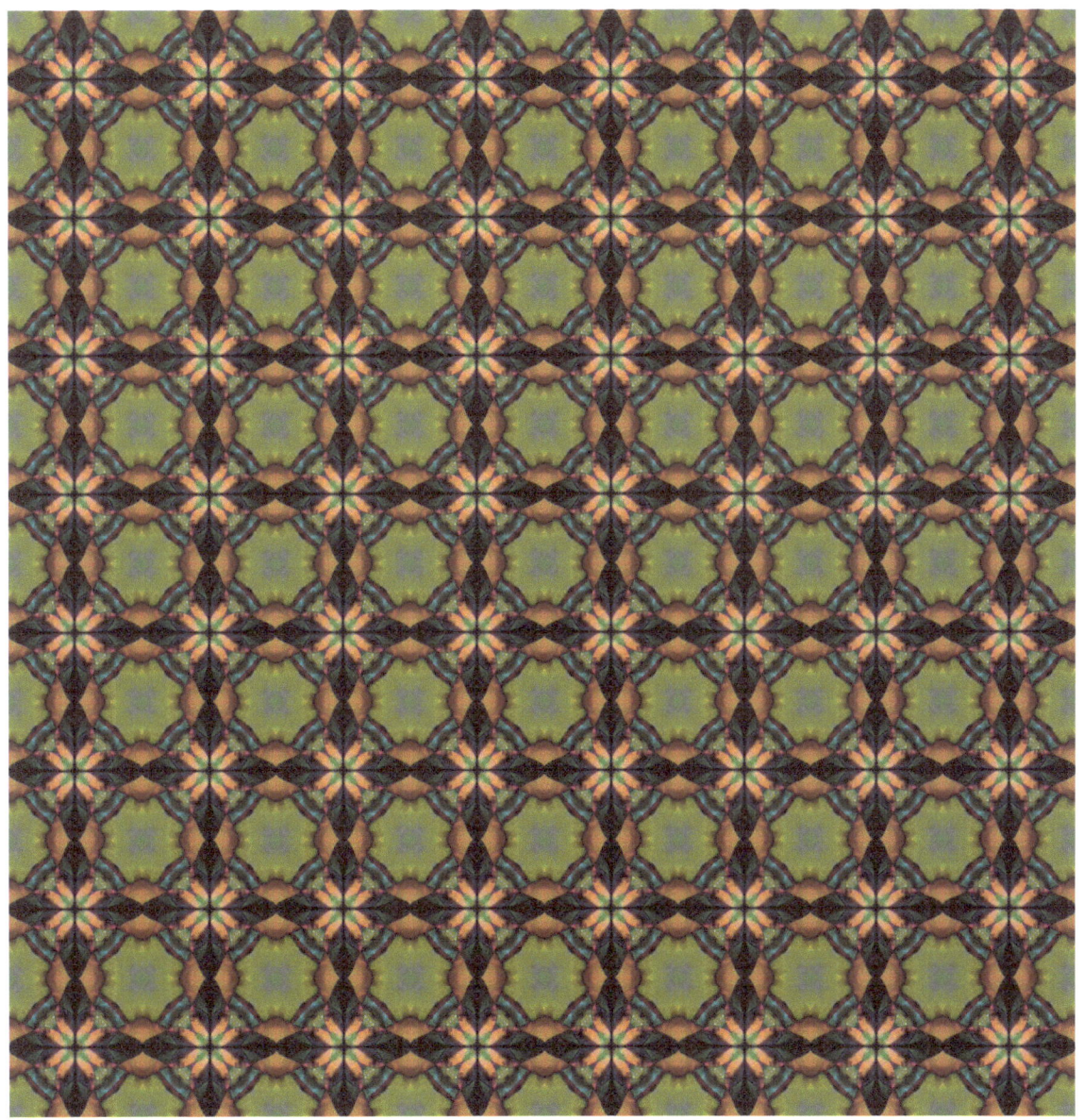

The First

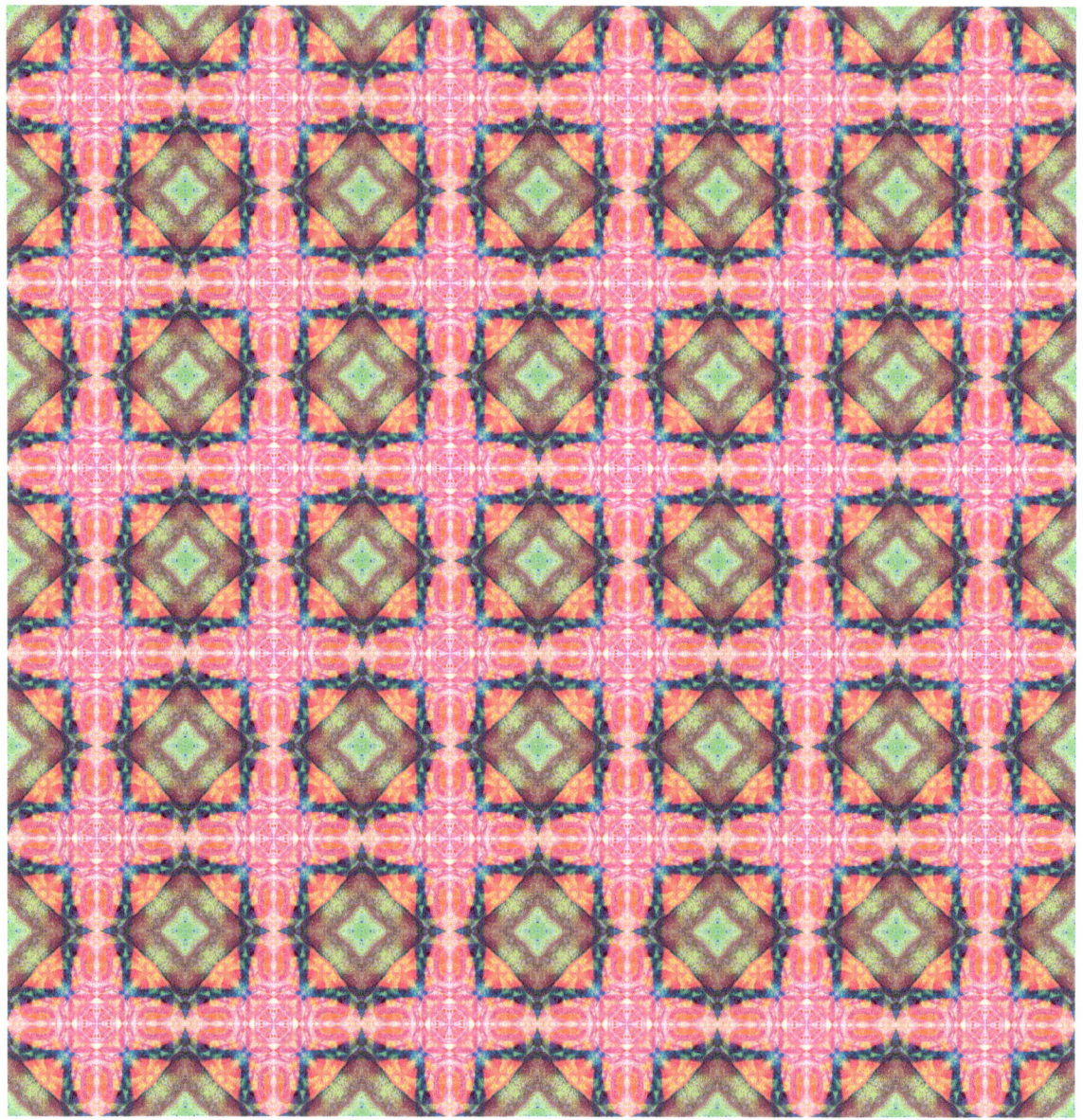

The Table

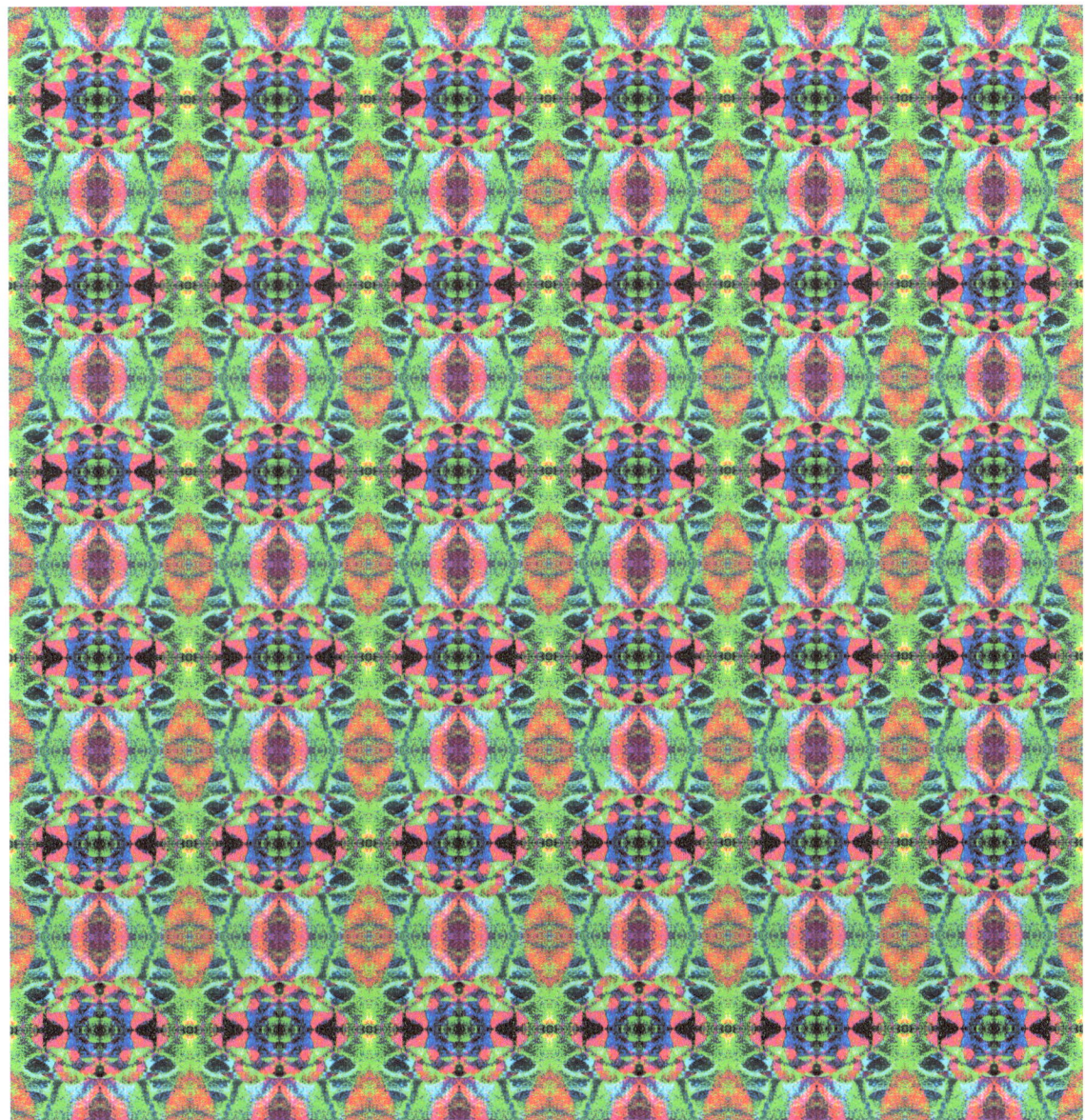

The Words

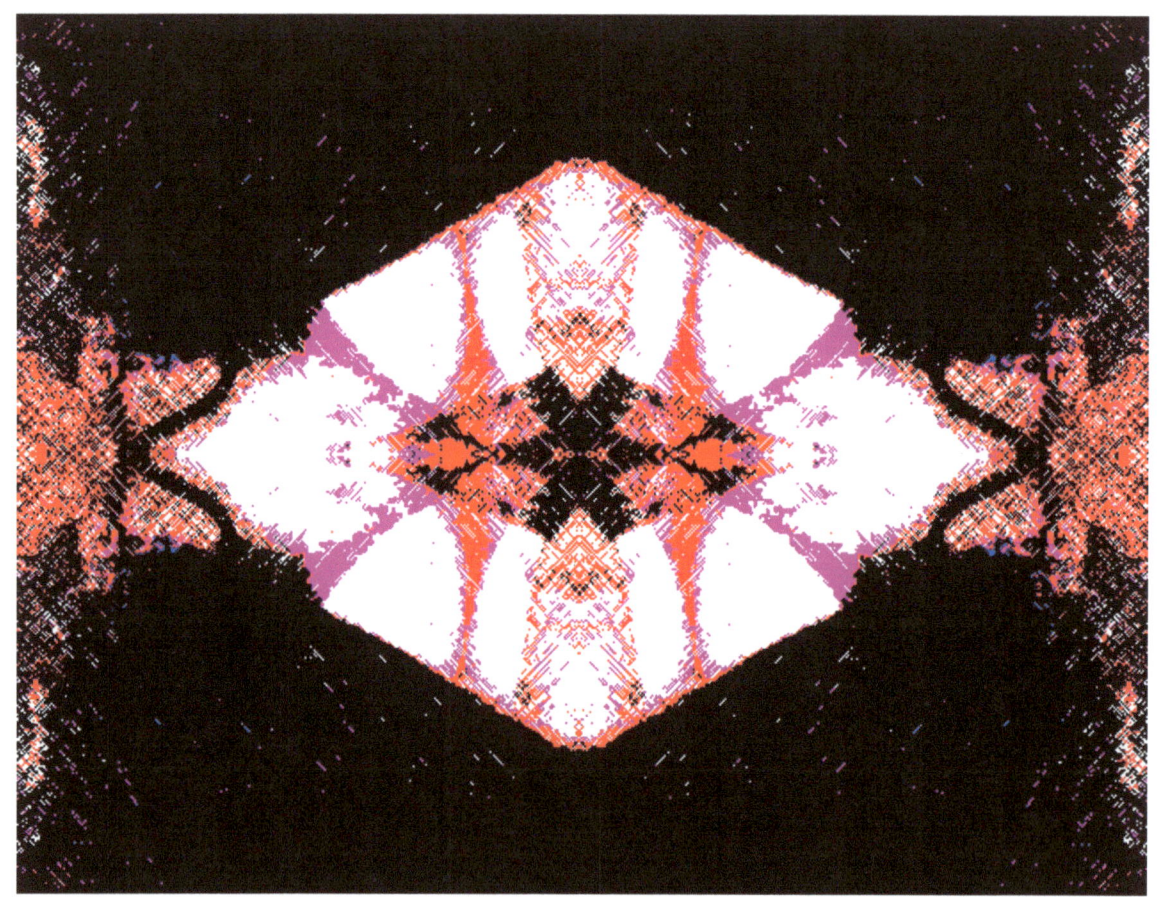

There With Me

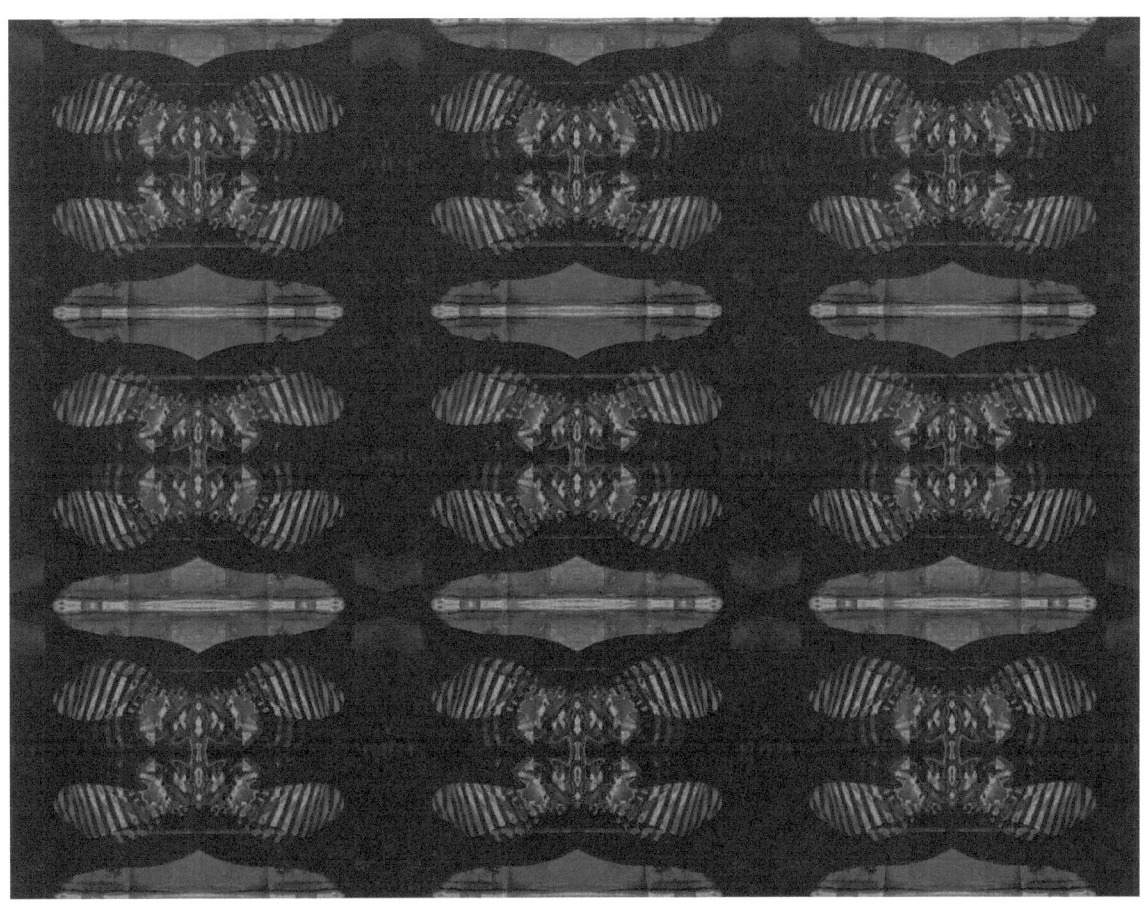

Thrown Around

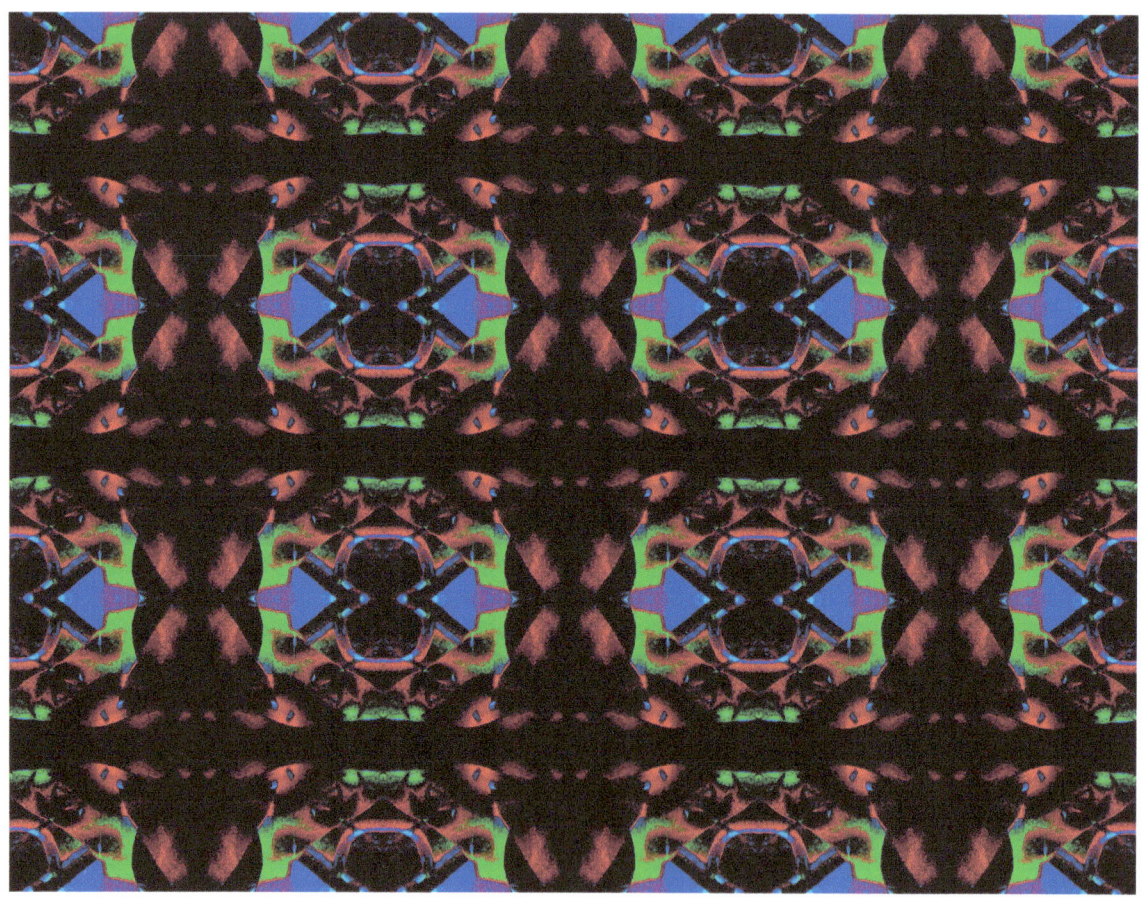

Til The End

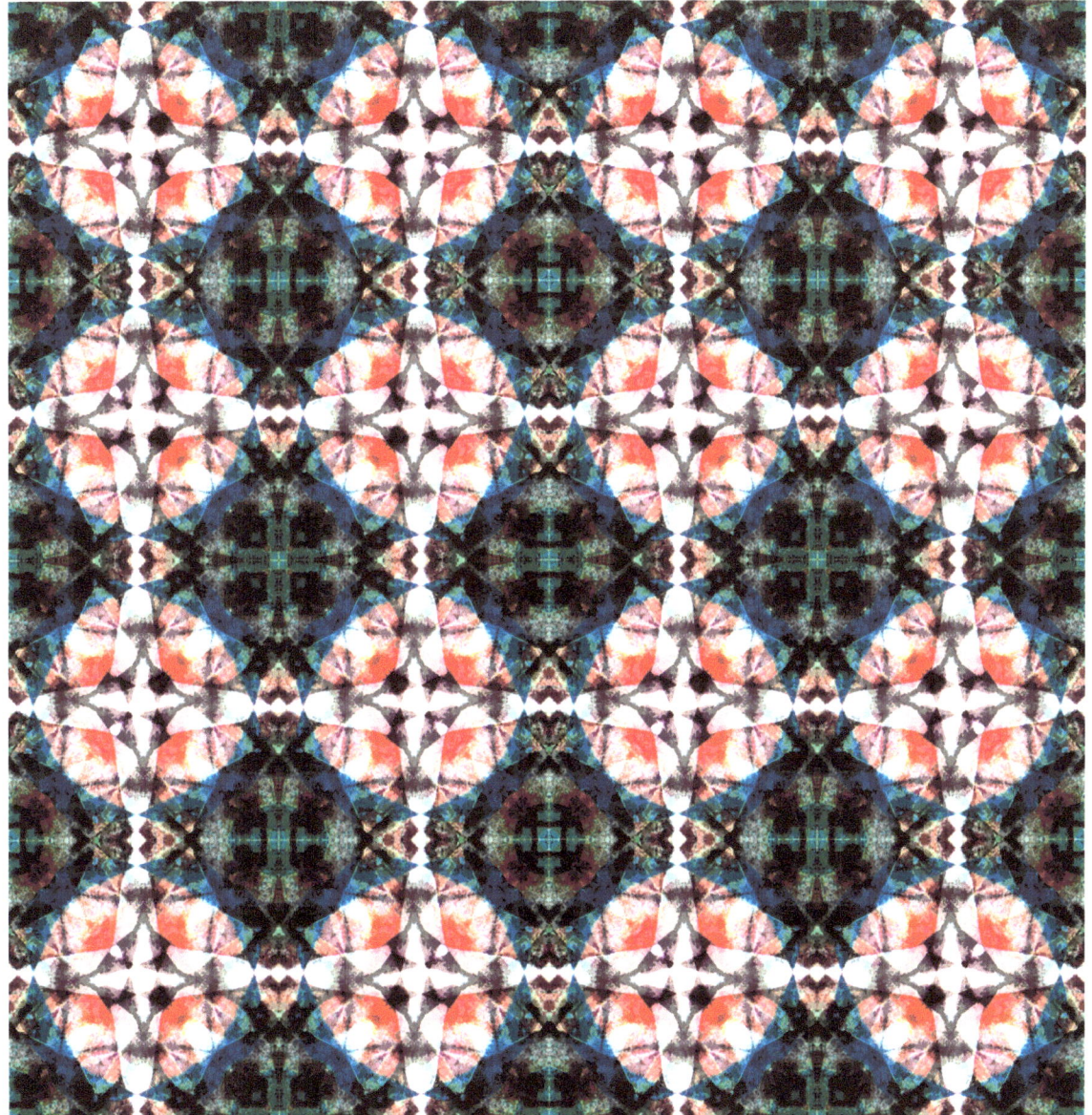

Trying To

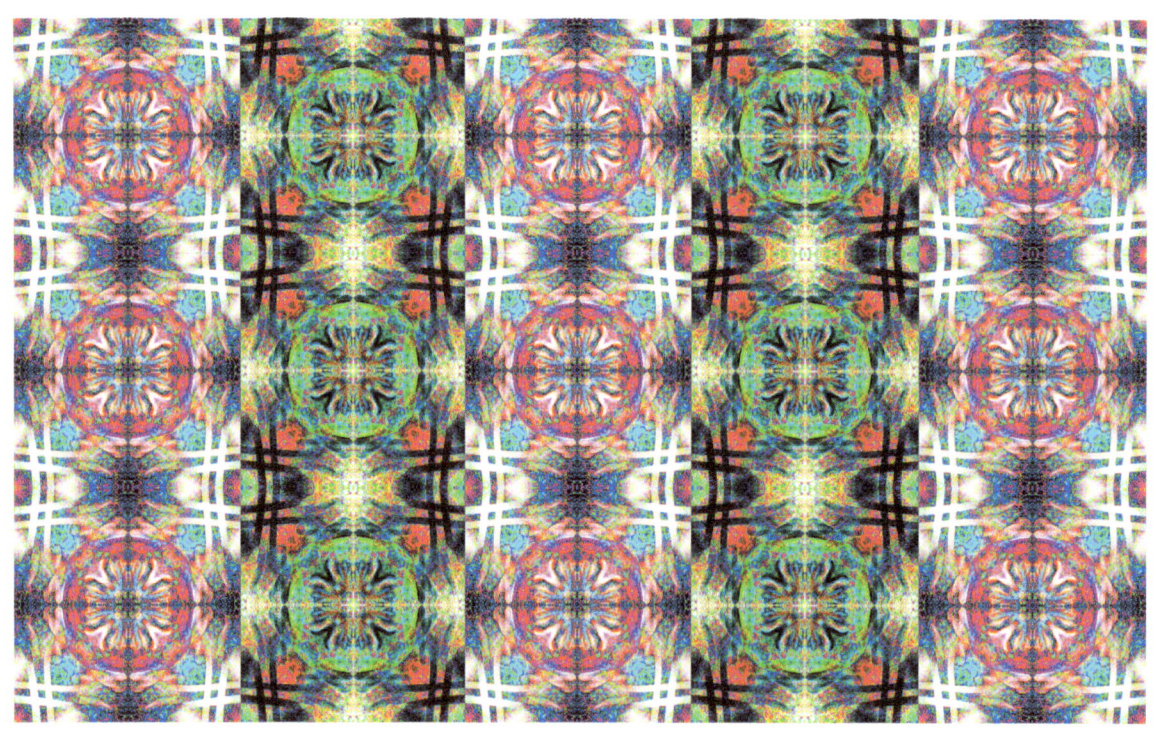

Utter Consentration

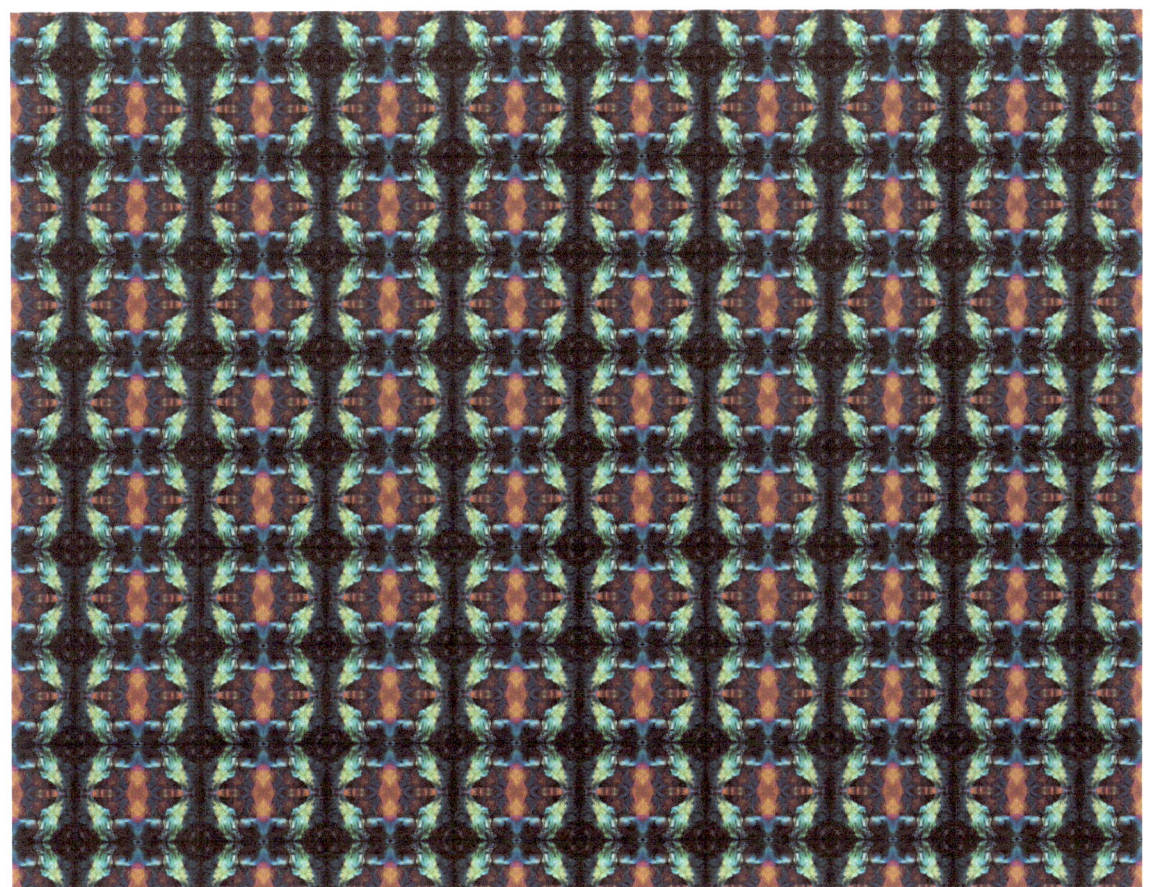

Very Happy

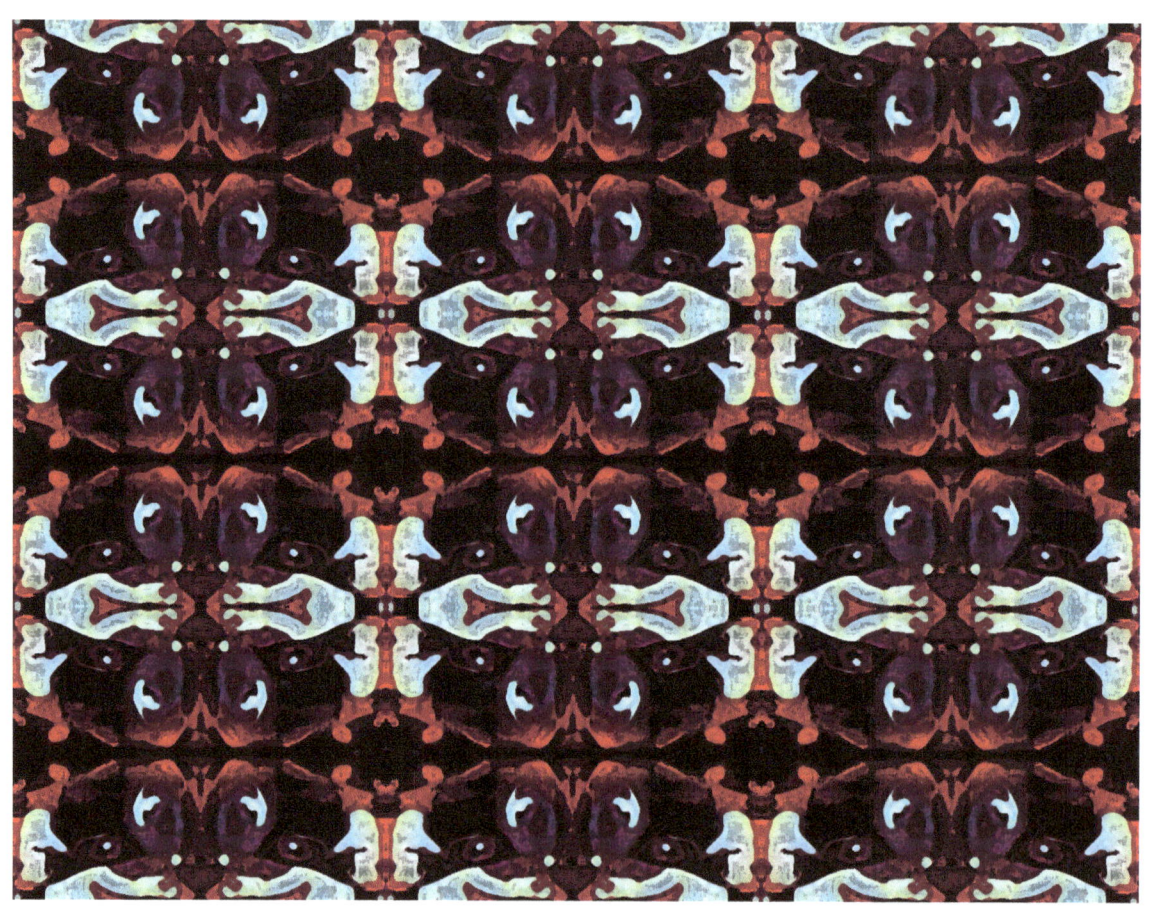

Want Anything

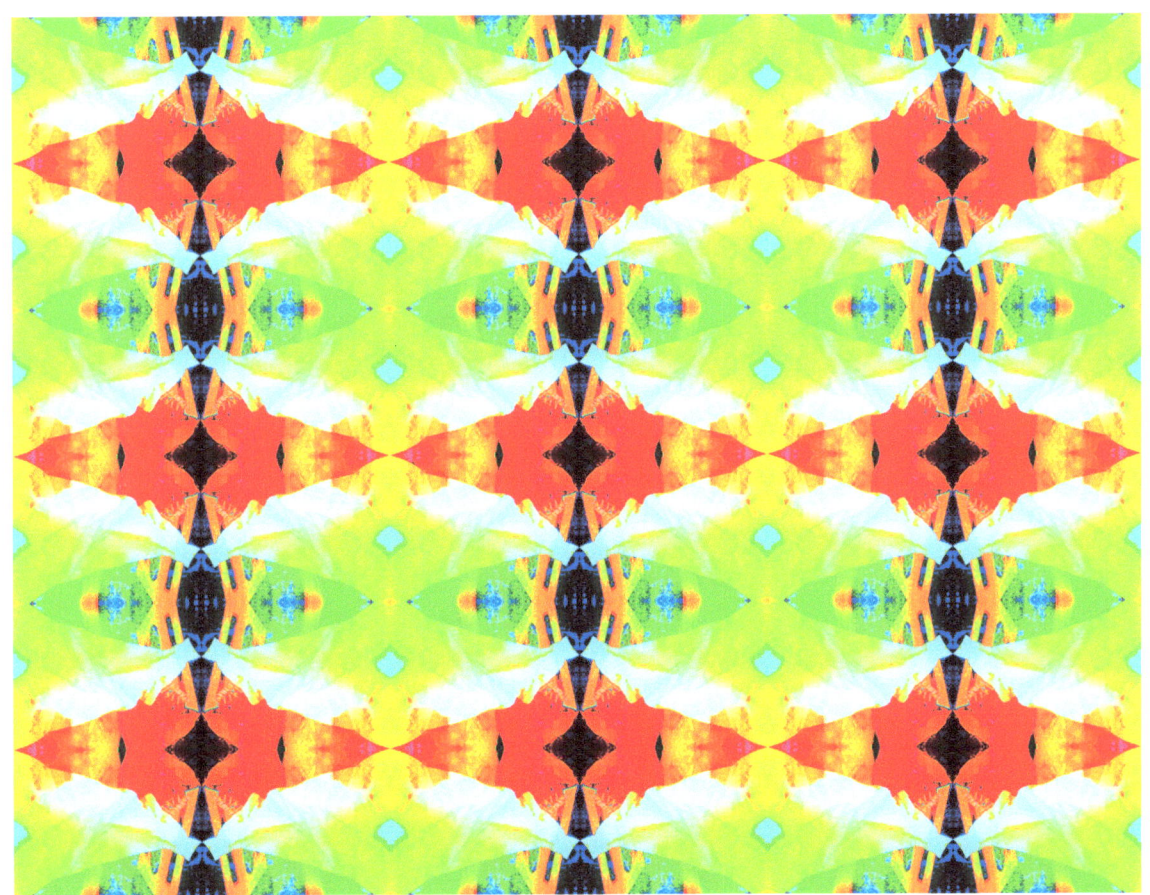

Way Too Much

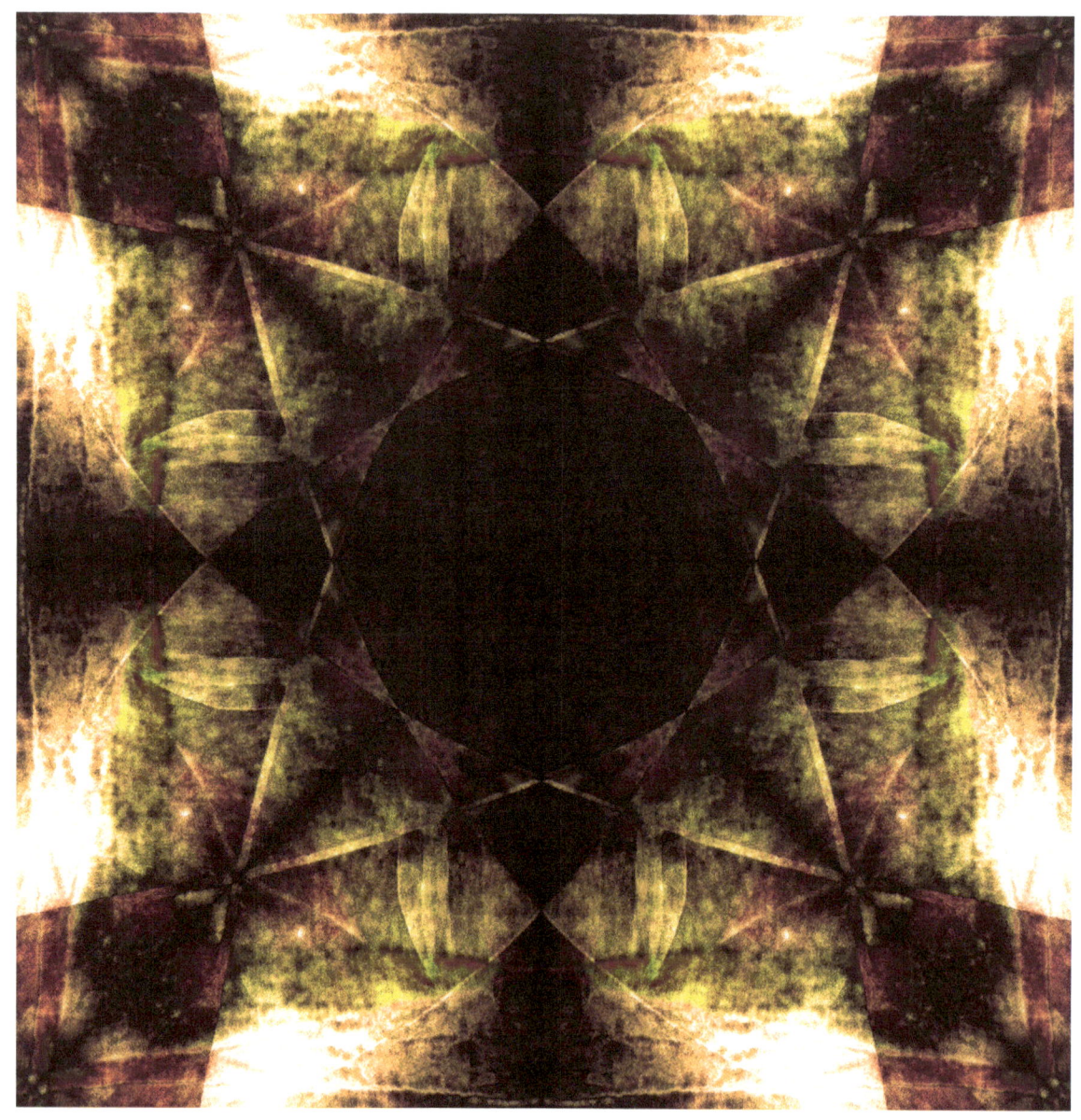

We Will

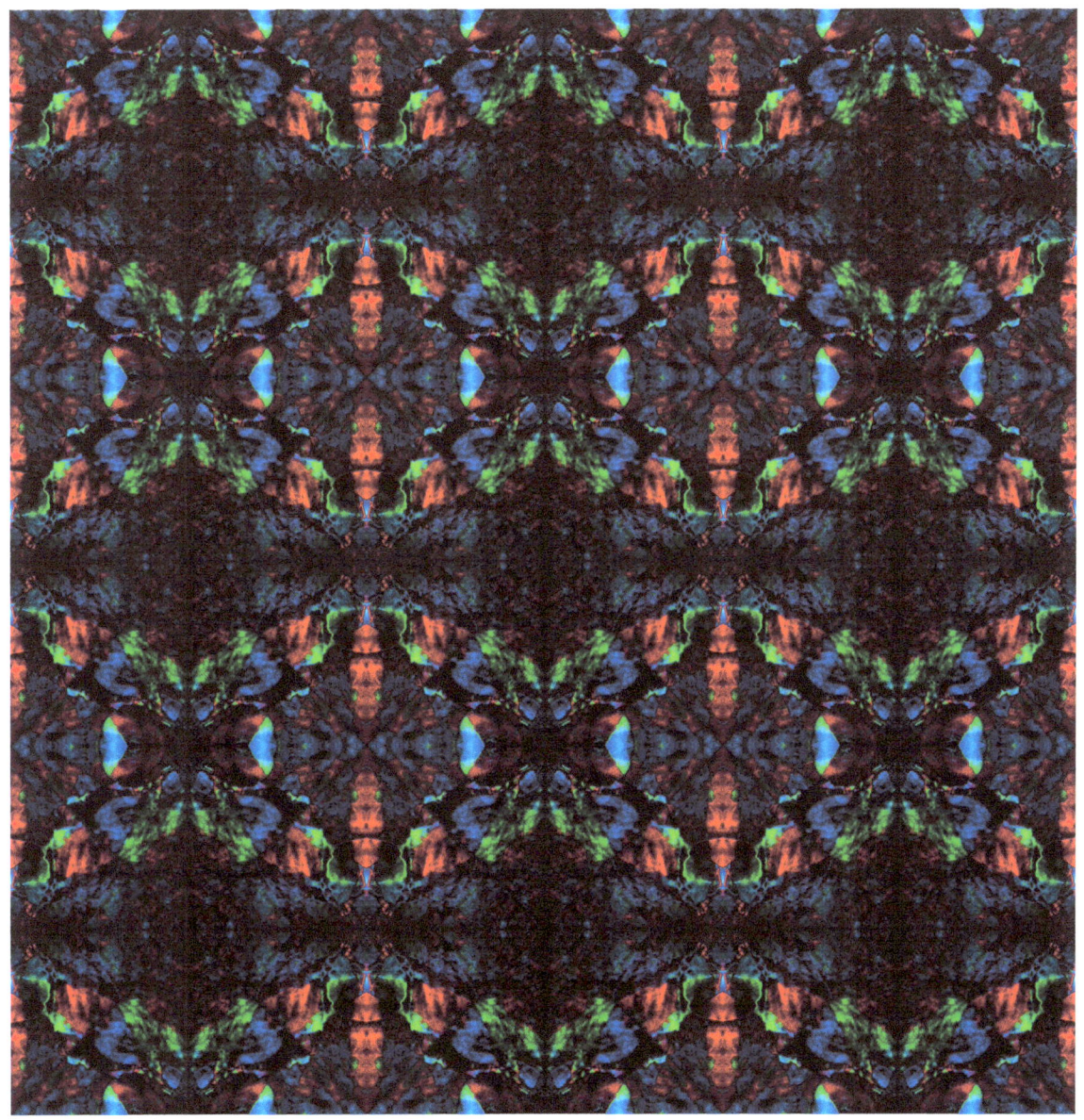

Woke Up

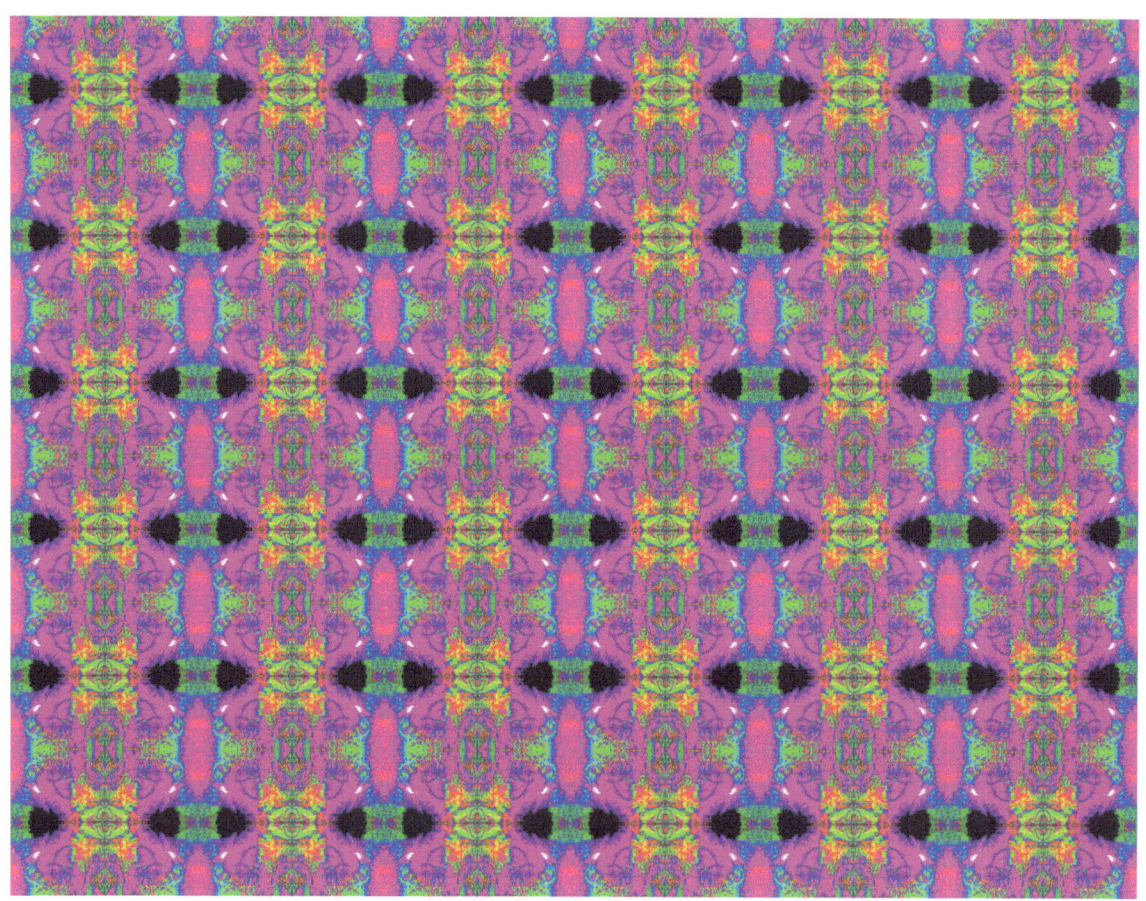

Yes

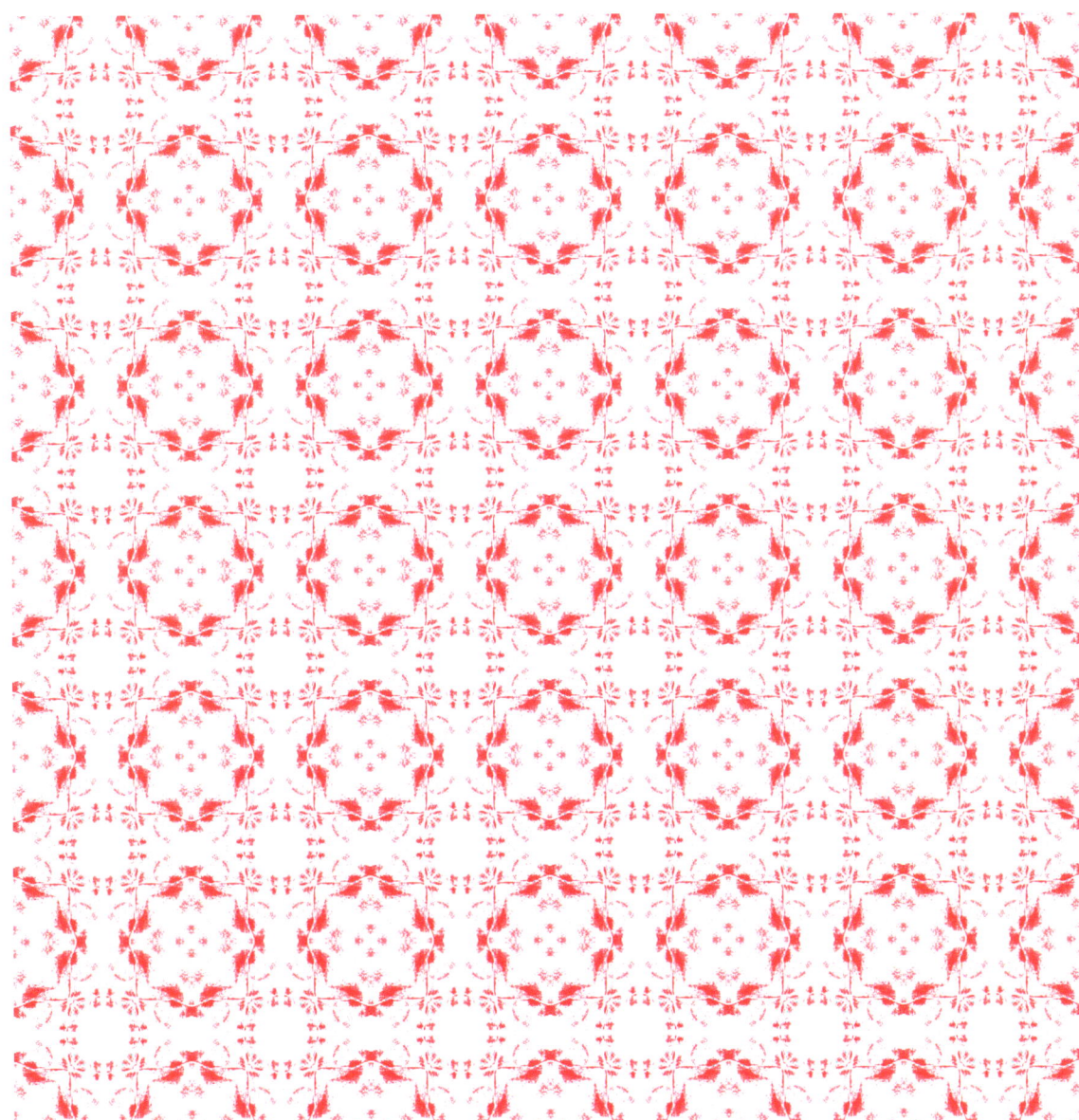

You Know It

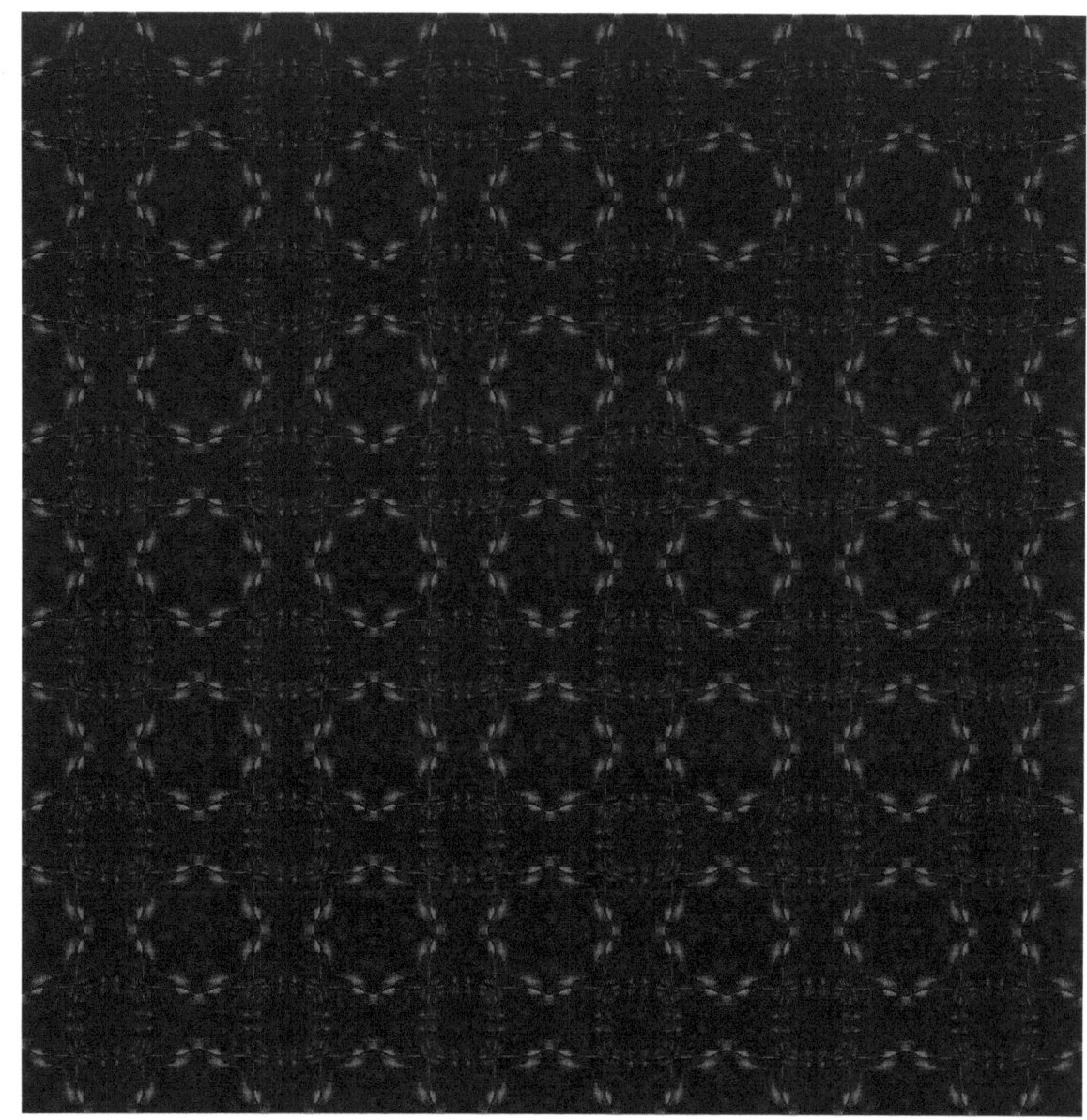

You Should

www.ingramcontent.com/pod-product-compliance
Lightning Source LLC
Chambersburg PA
CBHW050757180526
45159CB00003B/1494